Traditional Farm Buildings of Britain

Traditional Farm Buildings of Britain

R. W. Brunskill

London
Victor Gollancz Ltd
in association with Peter Crawley
1982

British Library Cataloguing in Publication Data

Brunskill, R. W.
   Traditional farm buildings of Britain.
   1. Farm buildings – Great Britain – History
   I. Title
   631.2′0941   NA8202

   ISBN 0-575-03117-4

Filmset and printed in Great Britain by
BAS Printers Limited, Over Wallop, Hampshire

Contents

List of Illustrations

Chapter 7

Chapter 8

Key to credits

Aerofilms: Aerofilms Ltd

RWB: R. W. Brunskill

PSC: P. S. Crawley

NMR: National Monuments Record

WGM: W. G. Muter

CFS: C. F. Stell

RW: R. Williams for Breconshire Education Committee

JAW: J. A. Wray

In this list and throughout the book the traditional county names and locations have been used.

Preface and Acknowledgements

As I mentioned in the preface to my first book on vernacular architecture I feel privileged that I am only one generation from the land. I was fortunate as a boy in having been able to spend school holidays on the farms of my grandparents, uncles and cousins and to take part in a way of life which only forty years ago retained intact many of the traditions accumulated over several centuries. It was during such holidays spent in what was then called Cumberland and Westmorland that I became aware of those characteristics of the buildings of the farmstead which I was later taught were components of vernacular architecture.

While a student at the School of Architecture in the University of Manchester my eyes were opened to the potentialities in the study of vernacular architecture which were beginning to be realised by Professor R. A. Cordingley. He was himself of a farming family and saw vernacular farm buildings with a farmer's eye as well as that of an architect. He had realised that any study of vernacular architecture which was confined to domestic buildings would be incomplete and had already encouraged the work of D. C. G. Davies which led in 1952 to the submission of a thesis on the farm buildings of part of Shropshire which, as far as I know, was the first systematic piece of fieldwork completed in this subject.

My own work in the Eden Valley and Solway Plain had at first only touched on the design and layout of farm buildings, but with the help of a Neale Bursary of the Royal Institute of British Architects awarded in 1963 I was able to develop the study in those parts of Cumbria. A further award of an RIBA Research Scholarship in 1965 enabled me to extend general study of farm buildings to other parts of the country and to devise, with some difficulty and without complete success, a systematic procedure for recording the buildings of the farmstead.

During the late 1960s and early 1970s I was fortunate in being invited by D. Williams, Chief Education Officer of the County of Brecon, to take part in a scheme to study the farmsteads of the county and explain to the schoolchildren through their teachers what was of interest. I shared the task with T. M. Owen who considerably extended my understanding of rural matters through sharing something of his vast store of information on Welsh society. I was also able to learn a great deal from the local farmers who were kind enough to allow us to explore their farmsteads, and from some of the local teachers, including some who were themselves part-time farmers.

Progress in more recent years has been through working with my students in the School of Architecture in the University of Manchester. As undergraduates M. Boyett, M. D. Calvert, D. R. Moorhouse and C. Woodhead were among those who conducted surveys of farm buildings while among the graduate students

Miss L. Caffyn, R. A. Foster, W. G. Muter and P. Messenger worked on farm buildings. But it is to J. E. C. Peters and E. Wiliam, both of whom have made major contributions to published work on farm building design that I must pay the greatest acknowledgement. I have learned from all but from these two most of all.

Like all students of vernacular architecture I have learned a great deal from fellow members of the Vernacular Architecture Group, and especially its senior members, including N. W. Alcock, M. W. Barley, E. A. Gee, Sir Robert Hall, Mrs B. Hutton, S. R. Jones, E. Mercer, P. Smith, J. T. Smith and J. W. Tonkin. On farm buildings among those who have been especially helpful mention must be made of Mrs J. E. Grundy for information on Lancashire farm buildings and R. Harris for farm buildings generally and especially in Herefordshire and Sussex; I. Homes for work on oast houses, K. Hutton for study of horse-engine houses; D. L. Roberts for information on farm buildings in Lincolnshire, W. J. Smith for his wide general knowledge and specific work on barns in Lancashire, B. Tyson for information on Cumbrian building practices, B. Walker for his extensive knowledge of Scottish farm buildings generously shared, and Cmdr. Williams for information on Somerset farm buildings and kilns.

In extending studies into American farm buildings I owe a special debt to H. Glassie for many long discussions and much exchange of correspondence but I am indebted also to A. L. Cummings, C. Carson, J. Fraser Hart, T. Hubka, F. Kniffen, E. C. Mather and D. Yoder and to other members of the new but active Vernacular Architecture Forum.

Among colleagues at the University of Manchester I must thank A. D. Barlow for help with maltings, A. Ruff for the New Mills Survey, and R. B. Wood-Jones and the late T. L. Marsden for many discussions over many years.

As well as inspiring and guiding the book, Peter Crawley was responsible for most of the photographs and in thanking him and all the farmers who allowed their farm buildings to be photographed, I must make clear to readers that farm buildings are private, not open to the public unless so advertised, and ask that the privacy of farmers – and their livestock – be respected.

I must thank all the many farmers who have opened their farmsteads to me and have taken the time to discuss the history of buildings they are tempted to discard but anxious to keep. I must thank especially my mother and father, still with a feel for the land after over fifty years exile from it. Through them I must thank the many relations: grandparents, uncles, aunts and cousins, including those long gone, who, unknowingly, started me on the study of farm buildings and allowed me to use their farms for my apprenticeship.

Finally, I must once again thank my wife, Miriam, for all her help, especially with the typing, and my daughters, Lesley and Robin, for their continued forebearance.

Wilmslow, Cheshire
January 1982

Introduction

Until quite recently, most houses in the countryside were farmhouses. The medieval lord of the manor had his demesne land under cultivation; the Georgian squire had his home farm or land in hand; the priest with his glebe and the miller with his share of the townfields were part-time farmers; the miner or quarryman, the labourer or craftsman, though cottagers, usually had a cow and a pig, often several animals and pasture on which to run them, as a means of balancing the fluctuations in demand for their services. All these were in addition to the full-time farmers whether yeomen or copyholders, leaseholders or tenants-at-will etc. who comprised the great mass of rural society. Even in the towns there were residents who farmed surrounding land on a small scale and within living memory some of our largest cities provided the unlikely setting for large herds of dairy cattle producing milk of a freshness, if not always of a quality, which we cannot possibly expect nowadays. All these farmers lived in farmhouses but operated their farms from sets of farm buildings arranged in one way or another around farmyards.

Of recent years the study of farmhouses has developed apace and many books and many more articles have been written about them whether from the point of view of archaeology, building construction, folk life studies or architectural appreciation. Few books have been written about farm buildings though in number they far exceed and in variety they are at least comparable with the farmhouses they served. This book aims to provide an introduction to the study of the non-domestic buildings of the farmstead.

Study of such buildings begins with some understanding of the farming processes which they were intended to serve. The agricultural history of Britain has been long and involved and agricultural historians are even now far from unanimous in their interpretation of what records are available. Yet some broad understanding of the main changes in the development of farming may be anticipated and the farming history of the last couple of hundred years at least is becoming reasonably clear. An attempt is made here to summarise briefly the main agricultural developments, as they affect the design of farm buildings.

The three elements of the farmstead, farmhouse, farm buildings and farmyard were closely dependent on each other. The domestic activities within the farmhouse are well understood; the farm buildings in the past accommodated several processes and also housed several activities or functions. Each function may be considered separately. Sometimes each function justified a separate building, sometimes several functions were accommodated under the one roof. Since very few farms in Britain were ever purely arable or purely pastoral in their organisation, the functions related to the accommodation and processing of both crops and stock. Until a hundred years ago, and in many cases even more recently, farms were mixed farms with emphasis towards either cultivation of crops or pasture of animals. The fields were ploughed, the cereal and root crops gathered and processed, their products and by-products being used in large part for feed and bedding for the cattle and horses whose muscles pulled the plough, as well as for the sheep and pigs whose manure helped to fertilise the fields which were ploughed and sown once more. In examining a farmstead, one looks for accommodation for crops, for animals, and, in later examples at least, for the results of the processing of crops and for the machinery used in the various processes.

In varying proportions, therefore, one would expect every farmstead to give evidence of barns for the accommodation of hand or machine threshing, cow-houses and shelter sheds for oxen, milk cattle and young or store cattle, stables for horses, sties for pigs, dovecots for pigeons, houses for poultry, hay barns, lofts and linhays for hay, granaries for feed or seed corn and kilns, maltings and oast houses for the conversion of crops, implement sheds for carts and farming equipment and, on some farms, oddities like ash-houses for the storage of ashes before they were spread on the fields.

The building which we always associate first with the farmstead, and the building which was normally largest and often the oldest, is the barn and so a big proportion of the book is devoted to the study of barns. This includes the simple, once conventional, threshing barn, the larger aisled barn which so often served as a tithe barn, the later barns designed for threshing machines powered by wind, water or horses, and the last buildings recognisable as barns accommodating a mass of machinery and the steam or internal combustion engine to drive it. Occasionally in this country the designers of farm buildings echoed their fellows in other countries of Europe and America in concentrating other activities in a big, all-embracing barn and examples of these building types will be described and discussed.

Accommodation for animals normally spread wider than the barn and so the less imposing, but sometimes more decorative, cow-houses for tethered cattle, stables for working and carriage horses, pigsties and piggeries will be considered. At the same time the various ways of housing cattle loose in yards, open or covered, or in hammels or boxes will be described.

Birds were once much more important in the organisation of the mixed farm than they are in our modern highly specialised farming enterprises. The dovecot was for long quite the most graceful and generally decorative of the buildings of the farmstead, and even after separate dovecots had passed out of use the pigeon holes in the walls of barns or granaries allowed the designers of farm buildings a rare opportunity of patternmaking.

Until the recent vogue for silage-making, sweet-smelling hay was the vital element in allowing stock to survive and preservation of all but the most hardy animals could not otherwise have been guaranteed, so various buildings for the accommodation of hay will be described and discussed. Again, before it became a factory-based operation the conversion of certain crops into usable commodities was an activity of the farmstead, and therefore kilns of various sorts, including those for malting and roasting of hops, must be described.

These various activities and the buildings housing them were arranged around the farmyard and in relation to the farmhouse according to patterns which varied with the size of farm, which varied in time and which varied sometimes from region to region. Farmstead layouts are examined, including those in which farm buildings were scattered as satellites, cutting out unnecessary travel and double-handling, as more and more distant parts of the farm were brought into the intricate pattern of cultivation and grazing.

The farm buildings here are mainly those which give evidence of traditional practices. During the eighteenth century and especially during the nineteenth century there was great enthusiasm for designing, and only slightly less enthusiasm for erecting, the ideal farmstead. From Prince Albert down the social scale landowners vied with each other, sometimes to the dismay of their creditors, in this practice. Such model farmsteads are not described here but their influence can sometimes be seen to modify the traditions which developed over the centuries. Similarly the great ranges of formally-planned farmsteads designed by architects to complement their country-house designs are not considered, except insofar as they in turn influenced traditional designs.

Instead we are concerned here with the farm buildings which form an important part of the body of what has come to be called vernacular architecture – the architecture of everyday activities conducted by ordinary people according to traditions varying with different parts of the country. An important part of the regional and local variations in this, as in other branches of vernacular architecture, arises through the materials and methods of construction which varied so much from locality to locality in Britain until very late in the nineteenth century. Without attempting any detailed explanation of vernacular building construction, a short introduction to this aspect of traditional farm building design has been provided.

The barns and oast houses, stables and pigsties seem part of a permanent, never-changing landscape, the countryside of the magazine cover, the television advertisement and the Christmas Calendar. But, of course, the farm buildings are even more vulnerable than the hedges and hedgerow trees, the coppices and ponds which fall victim to modern farming practices. It is a testimony to the sense of history retained by a great number of farmers and landowners that so many traditional farm buildings survive long after their original purpose has been lost, even forgotten. Many farm buildings are demolished each year, many more are hidden behind the great sheds of air-conditioned, laboratory-like farming factories which commercial agriculture requires, but some are given a new life through conservation. Some are adapted to a new farming use, some are converted to community use or made into houses or workshops, some house the increasingly popular farming museums. The book closes, therefore, with a brief examination of recent trends in the conservation of barns and some other farm buildings.

The repair and adaptation of farm buildings is rarely cheap. But quite often it is cheaper than the construction of a new, less adaptable, building. Where the will to conserve farm buildings can be determined the way to do it can often be discovered. Greater understanding of the relationship between building and farming activity, between farmhouses and the rest of the farmstead will surely foster this will and true conservation of a significant part of our wealth of traditional buildings and the memory of the history which they enshrine will be secured.

Chapter 1

Farming history and the standard farmstead

The story of farming in this country as affecting the design of farm buildings may be allowed to begin with the Norman Conquest and the Domesday Survey of 1086. The story has, as its prologue, the process, conducted over centuries, millennia even, of settlement in Great Britain. Waves of immigrants and slowly expanding tribes of inhabitants created permanent settlements devoted to arable cultivation, to pastoral farming and the hunting and gathering of the produce of the still abundant waste land. Axes and burning brands had cleared much of the standing forests and nibbling sheep, goats and pigs had prevented regeneration. An economic balance had been created between man and nature varying from county to county and province to province; a social balance had been established between those who held land in some way and those who tilled it. The social and economic balance was to be recorded in the Domesday Book and merged into the balanced feudal system of social, economic and governmental organisation.

The manor was the basis of medieval agricultural life. The Lord of the Manor held land from his feudal superior in return for past benefits, present services or, in the case of the huge ecclesiastical holdings, in acknowledgement of intangible future benefits. Villeins, cottars, servile tenants of various sorts maintained rights in land in proportion to the services they rendered to their lord: regular services of so many days' labour on the lord's own farm, occasional services at harvest or during one of the great agricultural seasons, military service when required, compulsory use of manorial facilities, principally the corn mill. The various holdings as established by law and custom were set out in the Domesday Book.

The typical manor can be found no more easily than any other typical element in the countryside but many manors did conform to a pattern whereby the land stretched from a river towards the top of a hill. The river and its tributary streams and springs provided the water supply for man and beast, it also irrigated by its frequent flooding the meadow lands in the valley bottom. These lands were held in common and provided the hay for winter fodder, the last bite of grass in the autumn and the essential first bite in springtime. Above the meadows were the open fields: two, three, four or even more, but commonly three great defined fields. Each field was divided into many narrow strips which formed the units of cultivation. Every farmer had the right to cultivate a number of strips according to the holding he enjoyed, and his collection of strips would be scattered about the fields in a way which gave him a fair share of good and bad land, wet and dry conditions, stony and clear soil, steep and flat slopes and a fair share of exposure to the sunshine. In many manors it was the custom to make a fresh distribution of strips each year, in others, and eventually in most, the allocation was fixed. Each strip represented a work unit, often the amount of

1. **Aerial view of a farmstead in Cornwall** (Aerofilms) The farmhouse is detached, the buildings scattered and there is a horse-engine house attached to the barn.

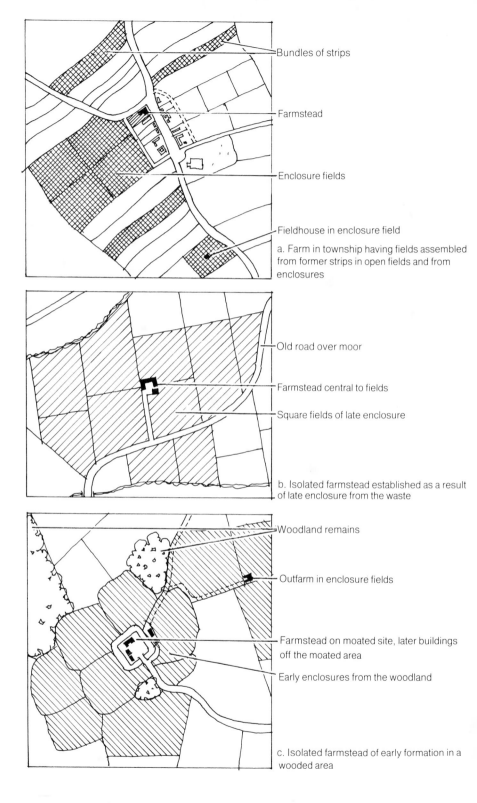

Bundles of strips

Farmstead

Enclosure fields

Fieldhouse in enclosure field

a. Farm in township having fields assembled from former strips in open fields and from enclosures

Old road over moor

Farmstead central to fields

Square fields of late enclosure

b. Isolated farmstead established as a result of late enclosure from the waste

Woodland remains

Outfarm in enclosure fields

Farmstead on moated site, later buildings off the moated area

Early enclosures from the woodland

c. Isolated farmstead of early formation in a wooded area

2. Farmstead locations

land which could be ploughed in a day and the size of unit varied with the quality of the land and the local farming practices. Each strip was the shape of a slightly reversed S on plan and was slightly domed on section, both forms derived from the use of the heavy ox-drawn plough. Bundles of strips within a field were grouped together and there were grassy headlands where the cumbersome plough teams could turn.

Somewhere near the middle of the open fields was the village itself. It might include a church and a castle or manor house; there would be a green – rectangular, triangular or elongated as common land, and each farmstead site or toft was set in a larger plot or croft comprising farmyard, garden, orchard etc. There might also be some small enclosed fields or closes. Around the open fields and especially on the upper slopes was the common land or waste. This was used for rough grazing by the animals belonging to the members of the manorial community. Part would be preserved as the woodland for the village, providing, through carefully controlled felling, timber for new buildings and repairs, for fuel, and, by way of coppicing and pollarding, the wood necessary for village crafts and small scale industries. The community would also maintain rights for peat cutting or gathering outcrop coal for fuel.

Beyond the upper parts of the common land there was, in hilly or mountainous districts, a further zone which was common to several manors

3. Aerial view of a farmstead in Northumberland (Aerofilms) The buildings are arranged around a large courtyard serving as a foldyard; some round stacks may be seen in a stackyard behind the barn.

and provided summer pastures for the animals belonging to nearby – or even quite distant – communities in variations of the age-old and ubiquitous practice of transhumance.

In such a typical village during the Middle Ages farming was a co-operative activity revolving around the production of cereal crops, for grain provided oat-cakes or bread for year-round consumption as well as a poor, irregular but sometimes quite important cash crop. The type of grain varied from region to region: wheat in the south and east, oats and rye in the north and west, barley on its own or mixed with other grains according to locality. The grain was sowed in the various strips following repeated ploughing in winter or spring, was harrowed and weeded during growth, then cut with the sickle at harvest time to be dried and taken for threshing, winnowing and, for the most part, milling before consumption. Yields were very low. On average for every grain of corn scattered as seed on the land there was only a three to five-fold return. Seed for the following year had to be kept back and so the net return was even smaller; large areas of land had to be sown in order to produce a return even at subsistence level. As the fertility of the soil was low (and probably reducing during the medieval period) continuous cropping was impossible and whole open fields had to be allowed to revert to fallow for, say, one year in three, or even for each alternate year.

The arable fields were cultivated with the aid of teams of oxen: a yoke or two on light sandy soil, four, six or eight oxen yoked together for ploughing heavy clay lands. Few farmers had more than a pair of oxen and so cultivation was a co-operative business, yokes being added together to make up the required teams. The ox, though slow-moving and clumsy in use, was stolid and not particularly temperamental, was undemanding in his diet, had quite a long working life and produced meat and skin for leather-making when slaughtered. Small numbers of cows were also kept for breeding, to provide milk for cheese making and, again, produced meat and skins. Sheep were more numerous and an equally indispensable part of medieval agricultural economy, providing wool milk, meat and, above all, manure. Sheep grazing the pastures and then folded at night on arable land during winter provided what little fertiliser the cornlands enjoyed. Pigs and goats were also kept but herded on the waste rather than confined in the farmyard.

Administration was under the control of the Lord of the Manor or his representative but day-to-day operations were in the hands of nominated or elected members of the farming community. There was the hayward, the forester, the swineherd etc. The rights and duties of each member of the community were established by custom as much as by statute and were enforced and modified in the manorial courts.

The typical manor, insofar as it could be isolated, of a nucleated village on an ideal site was in any case only typical of midland and eastern counties of England. It was subject to many variations elsewhere. In Scotland and the northern counties of England, for instance, the infield/outfield or run-rig system was employed. There were one or two infields or townfields, divided into strips but receiving all the manure available. At the same time sections of the outfield or common land were ploughed, cultivated for a year or two, then left for fallow, allowed to grass over, reverted to the waste and then were ploughed up again

4. Farmstead near Crieff, Perthshire Isolated on a hill in wild countryside, the farmstead includes a conical roofed horse-engine house.

after seven to ten years. In some heavily wooded regions the nucleated system of settlement never became properly established, instead families cleared land from the woods, gradually creating a set of small enclosed fields. In much of Wales the pattern of village life and communal cultivation broke down early. Constant subdivision of land holdings among sons meant that farms became uneconomical in size while abundant under-utilised waste land gave enough opportunity for colonisation. So ancient villages in Wales tended to shrink into two or three farmsteads gathered near a church while hamlets of similar size or single large farms were established on the higher, and initially less attractive lands.

Few farm buildings survive to demonstrate the organisation of the early medieval farmstead. There are great monastic tithe barns still to be seen but they were not typical and even then the proportion of examples surviving is very small. Otherwise we have to rely on excavations, particularly of deserted medieval villages. Here again, although the buildings revealed are small and apparently simple, the many layers of short-lived structures, occasional and as yet inexplicable changes in alignment and lack of identifiable artefacts make interpretation difficult. So at the moment archaeologists can say little more than that peasant farmsteads consisted often of only two buildings, one a longhouse for accommodation of family and cattle and the other a barn for the grain crops.

The catastrophe of the Black death in 1348–9 had many social and economic consequences, some of which may briefly be mentioned: change in the balance of power between landlord and tenant, change in the balance of cultivation between labour-intensive arable and more capital-intensive pastoral, change in the distribution of population from overcrowded villages tightly packed on the best land to a more loose and open distribution, and the beginnings of a change in balance between land mainly held in strips in open fields and land mainly held in compact parcels enclosed in fenced fields.

The great reduction in population caused by this plague meant that surviving landlords lost the revenues previously brought by tenants constantly increasing in number and making demands on limited supplies of land. Now fewer tenants could work larger areas of land on more favourable terms which they could hope to dictate. More tenants could aspire to yeoman status.

Since primitive cultivation required many hands and many draught animals the reduced population was more productively employed in tending cattle, sheep and pigs grazing not only the waste but also abandoned open fields. Demand for wool for export and for home use remained buoyant. Nevertheless it is easy to exaggerate the change in balance between pastoral and arable farming: grain crops were still needed and the benefit of manure on arable lands was still to be sought.

While widespread grazing of formerly arable fields took place the pattern of ridge and furrow in strips lost its meaning. As the balance of grazing and cultivation was readjusted following the recovery of population from the Black Death so new compact fields could be established over wholly abandoned manors or in former parts of shrunken villages.

With the coming of the sixteenth century an increasing population was again pressing on the available land. We see this in Elizabethan worries about encroachment of cottagers on the waste and efforts to see that such encroachment as was permitted was in units big enough for viability: the four acres and a cow of the cottager.

There is no more evidence of the form of farm buildings for the period of a couple of centuries after the Black Death than before. Examples of the barns of monasteries or, occasionally, of great nobles do survive here and there but they do not tell us of the family farmer's stock of buildings.

During the Elizabethan period the population was growing at what, for the time, was a rapid rate. There was some check towards the middle of the seventeenth century but afterwards the increase resumed, giving pressure for expansion of the cultivated area and increased efficiency on what was put to the plough. Although some occasionally starved, the population was fed and industry, largely based on the products of the countryside, was developing.

One aspect of change in rural life lay in the change in relationship between landowner and farmer. Many of the manors, especially in the south-eastern counties of England, developed a yeoman class of substantial freeholders, close enough to the land to understand how it should be farmed, large enough to handle sufficient capital to ensure what was, for the time, efficient farming; able to balance the fluctuations in farming with activity in other trades or industries and not yet cramped and hidebound so as to become an obstacle to improvement. Even more numerous were the customary tenants who had acquired much of the security of the yeoman though still subject to fixed but small annual rents and less predictable and larger fines on certain events. Tenancy as we know it was beginning to develop through the 'three lives' system whereby land was held of a landowner for the lifetime of three named individuals, usually at a fixed rent. The tenant could normally expect to have the lease extended by successive lives while the landlord could expect to negotiate a regular increase in rent as a condition for extending the term. Cottagers held a house plot or rather more and could expect a wage income from farming employers who, in their turn, could count on an adequate supply of labour from season to season in the farming year.

Another aspect of change in rural life lay in the expansion of the properly cultivated area. There were still large expanses of cold, wet, treeless uplands subject to limited grazing, especially through remnants of medieval practices of transhumance. There were still also large areas of mosslands, low-lying wet

5. Farmstead near Hebden Bridge, Yorkshire
The farmstead consists of a farmhouse and combination barn building but there are some modern specialist farm buildings. The setting illustrates the great square fields of enclosure on rather barren moors.

boggy land, often heavily treed, usually inaccessible, but to which unruly families of hunters and fishermen had established claims in custom if not in law. During this period, more and more of the upland was enclosed and divided into farms while more and more of the mosses were drained, the most spectacular enterprise being the drainage of the Fens.

The land, whether of new enclosure or old, was better cultivated. Probably the greatest improvement was in the development of convertible husbandry. Throughout the Middle Ages agriculture had depended on the balance between grazing animals with their manure and cereal cultivation with its need for constant renewal of the fertility of a limited amount of arable land. This had been seen at its best in the grazing of sheep on downland pasture during the day and folding on open fields for dung to be dropped at night. Now it became the practice to lay down a part of each farm to grass for a few years so that it could be manured by grazing animals and then plough it up for a few years and grow cereal crops until yields began to drop. Whereas a medieval farm might be half in permanent grass and half in permanent tillage (including fallow years) now, and especially in midland counties, about one quarter was under the plough at any one time, the remainder being under grazing and regeneration. The change was helped by improved seed and cultivation methods so that a tenfold yield on corn sown could be expected.

Another revolutionary feature of agriculture during the period from about 1560 to 1750 was the more scientific development of the old practice of allowing flooded rivers to irrigate meadows. Instead of depending on the haphazard, unpredictable and uncontrollable flooding of nature, meadows were laid with channels and with drains whereby water could be released for irrigation and flow back through drains to the river to be captured and used again downstream. A thin one-inch (25 mm) sheet of water floating over the meadows stimulated the growth of grass from roots fertilised by the deposit of silt. The increasingly productive meadows gave more and more grass for hay which meant that more and more cattle could be kept through the winter producing more and more manure for the arable fields. The meadows also had a longer season of growth, grass giving an early bite in the spring, growing to full height and weight in the summer and still actively producing 'fog' grass for autumn grazing.

From the late sixteenth century onwards the diet for cattle and sheep was improving partly through the use of clover but mainly through the introduction of root crops: carrots, turnips and potatoes. These amplified the supplies of food available during the winter months, they allowed the animals actually to put on weight rather than simply surviving and they gave some flexibility in feeding and manuring: sheep could feed on turnips in the fields where they were grown and drop manure at the same time, or sheep could be fed while exercising in temporary pasture land on turnips carted from the ploughed land; cattle could be stall-fed on these crops.

Again, improvements to agriculture, especially in the midlands and south, fostered improvements in the interlocking agricultural economies of different parts of Britain. Cattle bred on widely scattered pastures in the north and west were herded along the droving roads to fatten on the increasingly productive farms of other parts of the country before being driven for slaughter in the expanding towns such as London, Bristol and Norwich.

This first agricultural revolution has left evidence in the fields rather more than on the farmstead. Few sixteenth-century farm buildings survive though aisled barns in the southern and eastern counties of England were built at this time, echoing the form if not the function of the great medieval barns. Much more survives from the latter part of the seventeenth century. Many timber-framed barns and some stone-walled barns of this period can be found on the larger farms, especially in areas not subject to such complete modernisation in later agricultural revolutions. Some ox-houses, stables and dovecots also survive from this period. With the early part of the eighteenth century improvements were beginning to pay off and barns and other farm buildings from the period may be seen on quite small farms in quite remote places.

The Industrial Revolution with its spectacular heritage of cotton mills and steam-engines, dockyards and warehouses tends to overshadow the agricultural revolutions without which industrialisation of a small island with much barren land would have been impossible. The period from 1750 saw a growth of population at a rate quite unprecedented in this country. Much of that increase took place in rural areas but most of the people making up the increase were encouraged off the land through employment opportunities newly available in manufacture, transport, shipping and commerce, not to mention opportunities of emigration to America, Africa and Australasia. Until large-scale import of food became possible it was necessary to rely on a more or less static farming population to produce the greater quantities of more varied food demanded and paid for by a greatly increased total population. Improved farming organisation, improved use of farmland, improved farming processes, improved varieties of crops and animals and greatly improved farm buildings all enabled the farmers to perform this miracle.

The period was one in which a very clear economic and social tie was established between landlord and tenant. Landlords assembled great estates, often expanding original holdings with the land of yeoman and customary tenants who had found their farms suitable neither in size nor distribution of fields for efficient agriculture. Some of this land was farmed as home farms and many landlords set up model farms in which the very latest techniques could be practised and demonstrated. Most of the land was leased to tenants who paid high rents in return for leases which were long enough for security and detailed enough to set out the mutual obligations of landlord and tenant, the greatest of which was to maintain the land in good heart. The landlords now provided and then tenants benefited from vast ranges of new farm buildings.

Landlords and tenants jointly shared the benefits of a class of labourers and artisans. A still adequate pool of skilled agricultural labourers was even more efficiently employed in the countryside, but in the industrialising villages, towns and cities, never far from the countryside, lived artisans who could supply seasonal help on the farms which many still remembered from their youth. Between town and country and especially in the northern counties of England there were still great colonies of part-time farmers continuing to balance the day-to-day life and the cyclical fluctuations of a miner, a quarryman or a weaver with that of a small farmer.

The farms on the great estates were by and large more compact, more efficiently run holdings than their predecessors, largely as a result of enclosure. The amalgamation of strips in the common fields had been in progress for centuries. As each group of strips was assembled and taken out of any communal rotation it was fenced and cultivated as a close or field. As each section of common land was divided up by agreement among all who held common rights it became another compact, easily cultivated field. During the period 1750 to 1880, however, enclosure became a large-scale and formalised procedure.

Two sorts of enclosure took place on two sorts of land. The larger area enclosed was the waste land, the common pastures, potentially quite productive in the lowlands but quite unproductive in mountainous and moorland areas of the north and west. The smaller area was the remaining common arable fields,

6. Farmstead in Darley Dale, Derbyshire The farmhouse incorporates a granary in a wing, there are two other farm buildings as well as a nineteenth century steel and corrugated iron hay barn.

still found in strips and now divided into fields which were long and narrow but by no means as attenuated as the strips themselves. In one type of enclosure the majority of those with an interest in the land – landlord, rector and tenants as a rule – obtained a private Act of Parliament fairly to divide and fence the fields and to do this, if necessary, without the agreement of an obstructive minority. In another type of enclosure, use was made of a General Enclosure Act to allow this procedure at much less expense. As a result of enclosure it was sometimes possible to establish new farms each with a centrally located farmstead or to consolidate the fields so that old-established farmsteads were better located in relation to the total holding. One visible result of enclosure is the pattern of hedges and walls which characterises so much of England and Wales together with the design and distinction of farm buildings. The less visible result was the part played in feeding industrial Britain.

Enclosure of the waste represented one aspect of the extension of the area of land capable of proper cultivation. Another aspect was the reclamation of land from the bogs or the sea. The vast fields of South Lancashire and the Fylde, for instance, now so productive of wheat and lettuces, potatoes and carrots, were, a couple of centuries ago, dismal swamps above which a few clusters of mean cottages rose. Similarly, bays and estuaries throughout the coastline show where embankments were built against the sea so that the land behind could be drained and cultivated.

The increased acreage, whether enclosed or reclaimed, was better farmed than ever before. New forms of crop rotation were adopted whereby successive crops took goodness from the soil but replaced it by wealth of some other kind to be enjoyed in turn by a successive crop. Probably the best-known of these rotations was the Norfolk four course rotation of wheat, turnips, barley and clover successively, with sheep consuming the alternate crops of turnip and clover on the spot and so dropping manure ready for the wheat and barley.

The crops were taken off land that was in better heart than ever before. The heavy land was immeasurably improved by liming and subsoil drainage. Chalk and lime, burnt from limestone in fieldside kilns, broke down the clay into a fine textured soil gently releasing fertility to the roots. Subsoil drainage, made possible by the cheap manufacture of clay drain tiles and the ingenious use of special drainage ploughs, channelled away the surface water and prevented the formation of sticky mire in winter or hard-packed pan in summer. The light land was more and more improved by the addition of marl, clay dug from pits and spread on the soil; it was an old practice revived in the eighteenth century.

Fertility of the soil was maintained by several different forms of manuring. One way, as we have seen, was to continue the practice of having crops consumed on the spot so that manure could be deposited to be ploughed into the ground as part of crop rotation. Another way was to have manure trodden into straw in cow-house and farmyard to be spread each spring and, again, ploughed into the soil. A third way was to add imported manure. At first this was guano, bird dung which had accumulated on the islands of the southern hemisphere over many centuries and was now shipped to Britain to be spread on the land. Phosphates were also imported and incorporated in the tilth. Eventually, artificial fertilisers were to give still more potential to the land, the real capital of the farm.

7. Farmstead at Llanfair, Merionethshire This farmstead nestles in a slight dip in the ground on an exposed hillside near the shore. The buildings of local hard stone cluster together and have few and small window openings.

Crops of heavier weight than ever before were gathered with the aid of better machinery and farming implements. Horses had by this time almost completely superseded oxen as draught animals. They were now used to pull improved models of plough and harrow as well as grass-cutting and corn reaping machines to new designs. Horse-powered elevators loaded the crops and four-wheeled wagons transported them. Steam power was used on the farmstead but not in the fields, except in East Anglia where engines pulled cables to haul huge ploughs cutting four furrows at a time.

Animals shared in the agricultural revolution of 1750–1880. Improved breeds of horses provided power for the farm. Improved breeds of sheep and pigs played their part in producing crops of wool and meat for sale. But the most spectacular results came from improved breeding and controlled feeding of cattle. Contemporary prints show ideal cows of grotesque proportions but the reality of skilful breeding was an animal which could produce prodigious quantities of meat or milk as intended, and of manure as required. Whether fed in stalls within the cow-houses or treading straw in open or covered yards the cattle made the vital link in the endless chain of cropping, consumption, fertilising and cropping again. This use of the cow as an eating, fattening, manure-producing machine was known as 'high farming' and, especially after the introduction of cattle cake, made the cow reach new heights of productivity.

Nineteenth-century transport improvements also worked in favour of the farmer. By canal came the limestone or lime to improve his soil and the nightsoil to add to its fertility. By rail came the guano and cattle cake while from the village goods yard departed cattle, sheep and eventually milk itself for consumption in the cities. Some cattle droving did continue but the cow which travelled overnight from field to slaughterhouse was in much better condition than the one driven even only twenty or thirty miles along the roads.

Farming of the period 1750–1850 continued to be mixed farming. The balance between crop cultivation and livestock rearing varied from year to year and from one part of the country to another. Price fluctuations continued to be

8. Farmstead near Stokesay Castle, Shropshire The timber-framed buildings are set around a foldyard; most are part weather-boarded and partly with stone outer walls. Post-war corrugated iron buildings have been added.

severe and there were farming slumps as well as booms. But on the principles of 'up horn down corn' and 'down horn up corn' a farmer could adjust his farming to his estimate of conditions, feeding more of his crops to animals when prices were low, ploughing up more well-fertilised grassland when cereal prices were high. When the great agricultural depression began towards the end of the 1870s it was countered immediately, and for about sixty years afterwards, with a change to pastoral emphasis broken only by the great ploughing campaigns of the two world wars.

The period of 'high farming' witnessed a great investment in farm buildings and many, especially in the midland, northern and western counties of England, date from this period. There were barns for the conversion of grain crops, cow-houses, yards and shelter sheds for the production of manure during winter, stables for the large numbers of horses needed to provide power on all farms, granaries for the storage of grain to be released for feeding, for market or for milling, cartsheds for the newly invented implements and wagons, and other buildings for even more specialised uses. Some of these farm buildings were organised and planned as model farmsteads, others extended and generally filled out earlier sets; some were huge plants of industrial size with many yards and ranges of buildings linked by tramway tracks, yet others were small compact sets under single roofs on newly-assembled or newly-reclaimed land.

Developments in agriculture in Scotland followed a different pattern from that in the rest of Great Britain, there being two main geographical divisions and two main phases. The two divisions were the Highland and Lowland, the former including the mountainous areas of the north and west as well as the islands off the west coast, the latter consisting of the broad flat lands of the eastern coastal belt, the central valley of the Forth and Clyde and the upland areas and fertile valleys looking towards Ireland and the west. The two phases were from the establishment of a fairly settled system of land-holding until the ending of the clan system after 1746 and from that date until the great agricultural depression of the end of the 1870s, after which there was a great similarity in agricultural development between the two kingdoms.

Like England and Wales, Scotland was a heavily forested country before the arrival of the first farmers, but the forest had a greater proportion of coniferous trees and left bare mountain tops above and wide tracts of natural meadowland below. The spread of cultivation meant the loss of trees in the valleys, the spread of cattle grazing meant the loss of saplings and the lack of regeneration on the higher lands. Industrial development from the seventeenth century through to the early nineteenth century was at the expense of vast tracts of forest cut down to provide fuel for the furnaces. The remaining forests in the most inaccessible Highlands were burnt and over-grazed in the extension of sheep runs during the early nineteenth century. The bare hills and ragged mountains of Scotland illustrate a more extravagant use of limited natural resources than the more careful patchwork of the English counties.

Having stemmed the Norman invasion, Scotland never fell completely under the feudal system, though there was much Norman influence, both direct from the Continent and by way of England, during the medieval period. There was also a long-continuing Norse influence especially in northern and western parts. The nearest equivalent to the English manor in most of Scotland was the *fermtoun* or *clachan*, a hamlet with between about three and eight families farming communally according to the infield/outfield or run-rig system. The land so farmed was on the lower slopes of the hills, below the *head-dyke*, a hedge, bank or wall which indicated the limit of cultivation. The arable land was divided between an infield, located near the group of farmsteads, continuously manured and cropped, and extending to about one-fifth of the area, and an outfield lying between the infield and the head-dyke and occupying the remaining four-fifths. The infield was divided into strips about twenty to thirty feet wide (6.1 m to 9.1 m), rented annually by the tenants from the *tacksman* who had a sort of head-lease from the landowner. The outfield was itself divided into two parts, the smaller being the *folds* and the larger the *faughs*. A small part of the folds was taken for cultivation each year; having been manured by folded cattle for one season the portion was ploughed, cropped for two or three years and then allowed to lie fallow for five or six years until its turn for cultivation came up again. The faughs were not systematically manured and, being the poorest lands of the outfield, were cultivated only very occasionally. Meadowland on the flood plain of the rivers and streams was cropped for two or three years and then left to regenerate for another two or three. Pasture land consisted of the fallow in the outfield and the high pastures above the head-dyke. By way of transhumance whole families moved with cattle to the shielings on the high pasture for the early summer, tending the cattle which grazed these poor but extensive lands which often lay far from the fermtoun on the lower slopes.

In contrast to the English manorial and parochial organisation the Scots had an agricultural system based on the fermtoun and a parochial system based on the selection of one fermtoun among several to act as the *kirktoun*, a shifting cultivation of mainly poor land and a system of transhumance surviving long after it had been abandoned even in the highland areas of England and Wales. There was a clan loyalty over much of the country rather than a feudal chain of duties and respnsibilities and a set of recorded manorial customs. In contrast also to the changes and improvements from the Black Death through the first and second agricultural revolutions of England and Wales, the Scottish system remained in operation until well into the eighteenth century.

There are virtually no standing remains of the old houses of the fermtouns, let alone the farm buildings, and one can do little more than speculate on the design of Scottish farm buildings as erected much before the late eighteenth century.

The union of the English and Scottish parliaments in 1707 marked the beginning of a period of rapid transformation of Scottish agriculture, occurring first in the Lowlands and the spreading to the Highlands after the subjugation of the clans in 1746. The infields and outfields with their unfenced strips and occasionally cultivated *rivings* were replaced by regular fields bounded by walls and fences. The small clusters of farmsteads making up the fermtouns were replaced by separate large steadings with groups of estate cottages congregated in planned villages. The loose association of the clan and the uncertain tenure of the tacksman and tenant were superseded by freeholds and long leases. Small-scale family subsistence farming was replaced by large-scale capital-intensive farming. In place of one complete fermtoun there might be only one highly organised farm. Generations of improving landlords poured money into clearing fields, fencing, breeding cattle and horses, and building. By the early years of the nineteenth century, fertile parts of Lowland Scotland, such as the Carse of Gowrie, became models admired by English landowners, and, later in that century, Scottish farmers experienced in large-scale and up-to-date farming were enticed to England.

Planned farmsteads were characteristic of this period. On the larger farms there was a house, two or three storeys in height, standing detached from two or three courtyards of multi-storey farm buildings; on the smaller, a one and a half storey farmhouse was axially related to a U-shaped range of single-storey farm buildings.

Improvements in the Highlands and Islands took rather a different form. In the broad valleys the consolidation of clachans and their replacement by single farms took place as elsewhere; crofts or separate subsistence farms migrated to the coasts while the hill land became sheep walks. The crofters supplemented small-scale farming on the small areas of good land with fishing, egg-gathering and the harvesting of kelp. The graziers took leases of the wide upland rough pastures but for grazing sheep rather than cattle. To some extent the highland areas had become over-populated in that the few people were still too many for the even fewer resources; the agricultural improvements led to depopulation, some moving to crofts on the coastland, some moving to industrial work in Scotland and England, some emigrating to America and the colonies. The islands, having fewest natural resources, remained closest to perpetuating the agriculture, the landscape, and, presumably, the buildings of pre-improvement Scotland.

The depression in the grain-producing side of agriculture in Britain as a whole during the closing years of the decade 1870–80 must have seemed at the time like just another fluctuation. Soon events proved it to be very different. The apparently limitless prairies of North America were now under the plough and many competing railway lines sped the grain to the ports and the holds of steam-powered and iron-hulled ships. The Corn Laws, having been repealed in 1846, left no protection to the farmer and the newly enfranchised town dwellers naturally intended to enjoy, without political interference, a loaf baked of even cheaper wheat flour than that produced by an efficient but highly-geared home agriculture. The invention of the refrigerator ship towards the end of the nineteenth century meant that the industrial worker could now enjoy meat from the Argentine or Australia alongside his loaf of bread from American flour.

Agriculture in Britain survived by stressing livestock farming, especially for

9. Farmstead at Farway, Devon The large farmhouse with its thatched roof and characteristic chimney stacks stands apart but close to the farm buildings. The small building on the right is an ash-house.

10. Farmstead at Stopham, Sussex The farmhouse stands completely detached from an extensive range of low-walled thatched farm buildings all set in a rich countryside of fields and woodlands.

dairy products. Swift trains now brought milk from all parts of England and Wales to London and other big cities, driving out of business the city dairy farms. Commercial dairies beside the railway lines processed local milk into cream, butter and cheese. Intensive pig-rearing and poultry farming brought a more varied as well as a cheaper fare to the factory worker's table.

Nevertheless, reduced profits from land in hand, reduced rents from land tenanted meant that the landowner had little enough capital left for further investment in buildings. The great Victorian farmsteads already had ample capacity for cattle and could employ as many labourers as were likely to look for farm work. So building during this period of sixty years was at a low rate and then of cheap structures of steel and corrugated iron which could be abandoned or adapted as further agricultural changes took place.

During the First World War, and especially during its later years, food shortages encouraged the ploughing of grassland. This was still an equestrian war; in spite of railways and traction-engines, motor lorries and tanks, most of the transport and even some of the fighting was still based on horses bred on British farms and fed on British oats. After the war the balance swung again, with imported grain and meat, and even pig and dairy products, reducing the proportion of home-produced food in the national diet to a very low level. Agricultural administration was, however, prepared for the Second World War and from the winter of 1939–40 onwards a great ploughing campaign restored the agricultural balance to a mid-nineteenth century level. Indeed, many

11. Farmstead near Marshfield, Wiltshire The five-barred gate opens onto a neat farmyard and a 'driftway' or roofed opening leads to a further yard. A small timber dovecot may be seen in the roof over the driftway.

upland farms saw the cultivation of fields in crops similar to those recorded on the tithe maps of a century before.

There was no agricultural slump after the Second World War. Shortage of foreign exchange encouraged governments to maintain a high proportion of home-produced foods. Some items, of course, could not be grown in Britain, others were worth buying even with scarce dollars, but many items were bred or grown on farms modernised with the aid of grants and subsidies. The farm of the post-Second World War period became a high capital/low labour enterprise. General purpose implements, especially tractors, abounded; other expensive implements needed for a brief but vital period were acquired. Grass was no longer cut and tossed and turned to make hay; some was cut and put in the silage pit, the rest was cut, turned and baled. Cows were milked in a variety of devices culminating – so far – in the carousel wherein the cows are slowly waltzed around so that the cowman need not take a step.

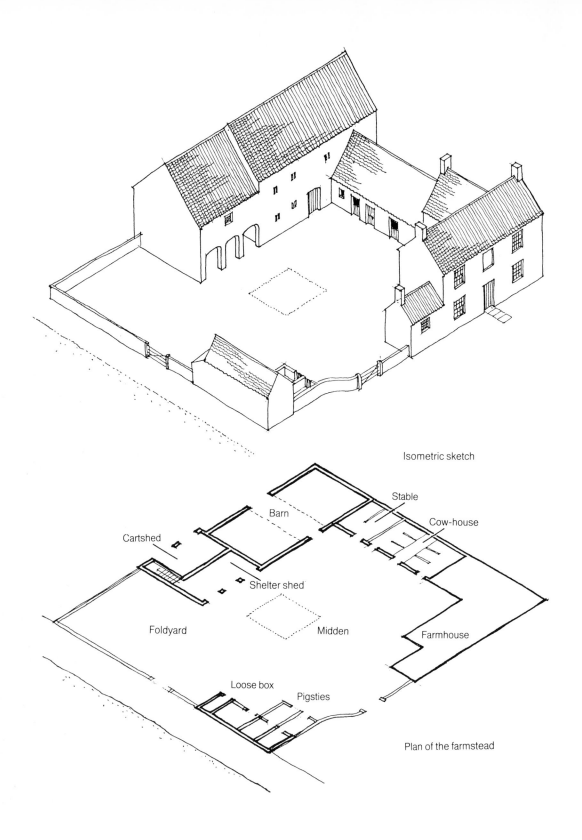

Isometric sketch

Stable

Barn

Cartshed

Cow-house

Shelter shed

Foldyard

Midden

Farmhouse

Loose box

Pigsties

Plan of the farmstead

The last thirty-five years has witnessed another boom in investment in farm buildings. Some have been general purpose buildings such as the huge cattle sheds, others have been specialised buildings such as the tall feed silos. All are of some technical interest but few are of architectural interest. In scale as well as in materials they so often seem foreign to the farms they serve. Meanwhile, the old farm buildings, whether rare relics of the fourteenth century or commonplace items from Victorian farming pattern-books, remain empty, and, at a faster and faster rate, continue to disappear.

The standard farmstead

Before considering the design of each individual farm building, or the ways in which various activities were combined in single buildings, or the various patterns in which the farmstead might be laid out, it may be helpful to devote a moment or two to the standard farmstead. This is intended to represent the farmhouse, farmyard and farm buildings erected for a family farm during the late eighteenth century or the early nineteenth century after the rude and ephemeral shelters of previous centuries had been replaced by permanent buildings. But it is a farmstead of the period before the increasingly scientific farming of the later nineteenth century led to the replacement of buildings well-built, but of traditional design, by others, sometimes even better-built, devoted to more specialised functions and more dependent on machinery.

The diagram (fig. 12) shows a typical family farm of about 1800. It is based on an example in East Yorkshire, but similar examples may be seen in the mixed farms of that period which abound in most parts of Britain. As well as the farmhouse, the farmstead comprises a barn designed for hand flail threshing of cereal crops, a cow-house for tethered cattle, a stable, a pigsty, a shelter shed, a granary placed partly over a shelter shed and partly over a cartshed, and all are arranged around a walled farmyard which also serves as a foldyard, accommodating loose cattle. Except for the cartshed which faces towards the fields, all the buildings face the farmyard. The back door of the farmhouse gives access to the farmyard but the front door faces the approach from the rest of the village. As a small family farm in the north of England, the farmhouse is closely related to the farm buildings, and in fact is joined to one of the buildings.

If we take this as a typical farmstead of a particularly important period we may then see what was the origin and use of each building type here represented, how each was developed and what were the principal variations. Not every farmstead includes every farm building type but most farmsteads designed for mixed farming, whatever the emphasis, include examples of these principal types.

12. The standard family farmstead

Chapter 2

Barns and the processing of grain crops

Introduction

Grain crops were grown in all parts of Britain at all times until recently, the crops varying between wheat, oats, rye and barley. Sometimes a combination of grains was grown, but whatever was the principal grain crop was called corn. The crops were grown for human consumption, for consumption by animals, for processing in the way that barley is converted into malt, and, of course some of each crop had to be saved for seed. The amount of cereal grown on any farm would vary according to fluctuations in trade, in the balance of farming and, over a long period, according to changes in climate. Yet cereals were grown everywhere and however unlikely it may seem to us nowadays the fields of the Orkneys, the Lake District, North Wales and Dartmoor have, from time to time, been just as much witness to waving corn as the fields of East Anglia.

Having been grown and harvested, the grain crop had to be processed before it could be used. There was a two-part process: threshing and winnowing. In the one the ears of corn were separated from the straw, in the other the useful grains were separated from the chaff. Sheaves of corn had to be stored at least temporarily before threshing and winnowing and the straw by-product had to be stored, again temporarily, afterwards. A barn is a building for the processing and temporary storage of the grain crop; it is more a factory than a warehouse.

Tithe barns

Many old barns are called tithe barns; in areas where really old barns are scarce then seventeenth or eighteenth century barns may be described as tithe barns. The term itself is a comparatively late one for the description even of true tithe barns. Such barns, however, do certainly exist and provide an exception to the rule that a barn is intended more for processing than storage.

A tithe is a tenth part of the annual profits from the occupation of land, from the run of stock upon land, and from the industry of persons occupying land. It was levied in this country from the ninth century as an ecclesiastical tax intended for the support of the parish priest. Such a priest was called a rector and as well as bearing the duties of care of his parish he also enjoyed the privileges, such as the collection of tithe. There were three varieties all originally payable in kind; personal tithes for example on labour, praedial tithes levied on the proportion of grain, hay etc. growing on land in the parish, and mixed tithes, that is on wool, milk etc. resulting from consumption on the land of crops grown on the land. Theoretically every parish would have a rector and a tithe barn in which the rector could receive and store his tithes.

In practice, many parishes had a rector who was not the parish priest. The rectorial duties and benefits might be in the hands of a monastery or college who would collect the benefits and provide a vicar to carry out the duties. Hence a monastic establishment might have several barns located in such parishes. After the dissolution of the monasteries lay persons often acquired the parochial parts of monastic possessions, became lay rectors, provided vicars but collected tithes, which, again, might be stored in tithe barns.

The largest known monastic tithe barn in Britain was that of Cholsey in Berkshire. It was 303 ft. long, 54 ft. wide and 51 ft. high to the ride (92.4 × 16.5 × 15.5 m) stretching for eighteen bays in length. Sadly, it was demolished in 1815 but drawings and a description of it survive. The largest barn of which some part may be seen is that of the Abbey of Beaulieu at its grange of St. Leonards, Beaulieu, in Hampshire. Quite a large late medieval barn occupies only a quarter of the floor area within the ruins. In volume, and thus in theoretical storage capacity, the Beaulieu barn was even greater than the Cholsey barn. The finest completely surviving monastic tithe barn is that of Great Coxwell, Berkshire, another grange of Beaulieu Abbey, and this is 152 ft. long, about 44 ft. wide and 48 ft. high to the ridge (46.13 × 13.4 × 14.6 m). It is the only complete survivor of the estimated twenty-seven barns belonging to that abbey. Indeed it is believed to be the only surviving example of between 2000 and 2900 monastic tithe barns belonging to the Cistercian Order alone.

Rectorial tithe barns are much smaller than those of the monasteries. They were built to contain the produce of the glebe land worked by the rector, or by others on his behalf, as well as the tithes of a single parish.

The payment of tithes had long irked parishioners, especially those of Roman Catholic or Nonconformist persuasions. By the Tithe Commutation Act of 1836, tithes were replaced by a fixed rent payable on land holdings. A century later, in 1936, tithes were virtually abolished. Even before 1836 many tithes had been converted into money payments and the need for rectorial barns had diminished; after 1836 many were demolished.

Thus we may properly study the comparatively few surviving monastic and rectorial tithe barns as buildings designed primarily for the reception and storage of agricultural produce and only secondarily, if at all, for the conversion of grain crops. By their size and antiquity alone they demand attention but in planning they tend to be marginal to the study of barns in general.

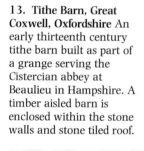

13. Tithe Barn, Great Coxwell, Oxfordshire An early thirteenth century tithe barn built as part of a grange serving the Cistercian abbey at Beaulieu in Hampshire. A timber aisled barn is enclosed within the stone walls and stone tiled roof.

Barns for hand flail threshing

The fields having been ploughed – perhaps several times to clear the weeds and harrowed and rolled to break up the sods – the corn was sown, broadcast at first, by seed fiddle later, and eventually with the aid of a seed drill. After more harrowing to cover the corn and some activity to scare away the birds, with any luck the farmer could hope that some of the grains of corn would germinate and grow.

When harvest time arrived all the members of the rural community would gather together to help the farmer reap his harvest. Some would cut the corn with sickle or scythe or, in the nineteenth century, with a reaping machine; others would gather the loose corn into sheaves to be bound with straw ropes made by their assistants; yet others would stook the sheaves into little houses of six, eight or twelve sheaves of the sort which once filled the harvest fields before the days of combine harvesters. Finally, when wind and sun had dried the corn the horse-drawn carts, followed by the gleaners, would travel round the fields gathering in the harvest with some ceremony as if the cycle of sowing and reaping had been completed.

So it had in a sense; the live grain of seed corn had multiplied and become the cluster of grains in husks on a stalk of straw. But sheaves of corn were not yet in a form which could be used by the farmer. Ears, chaff and straw had to be separated; first storage then threshing and then winnowing had to be completed.

The sheaves were stored either in the barn or in a stack or rickyard near to the barn. While yields were low it was common to put the whole of the crop into the barn at one time. The great barns of the monastic granges and the long and wide secular barns one can see as holding the full crop of an average season. The great cruck-framed barns of the midland and northern counties on farms large and small were capacious and some of the Reports to the Board of Agriculture condemned the practice of embarning the whole crop, as it survived at the beginning of the nineteenth century, as being wasteful of building space. When yields became greater the sheaves were made into stacks or ricks, rectangular or circular according to regional preference, thatched with straw and so protected until the time came for the ricks to be broken up, one by one to be taken into the barn for temporary storage before threshing.

The threshing process was intended to loosen the grains of corn and separate them from the stalks. Four main ways had been used in the past before the process was mechanised; having oxen or other animals tread out the corn, using an ox-drawn sledge to separate the corn, beating each individual sheaf on a wall or ledge until the grains drop out, and using a hand flail to thresh or beat out the grain. The first two processes have long been abandoned in this country though still used in parts of Africa and Asia; the third was only suitable for very small quantities though it has been used here within living memory; the fourth was the normal method, at least from the medieval period almost to the middle of the nineteenth century, survived in occasional use until a generation ago and is now being revived for demonstration in museums and at farm shows.

Hand flail threshing was a monotonous, dusty, arduous, generally unpleasant and unpopular task which had to be done day after day throughout the winter months. It required adequate space, light, height and controlled

14. Barns for hand flail threshing

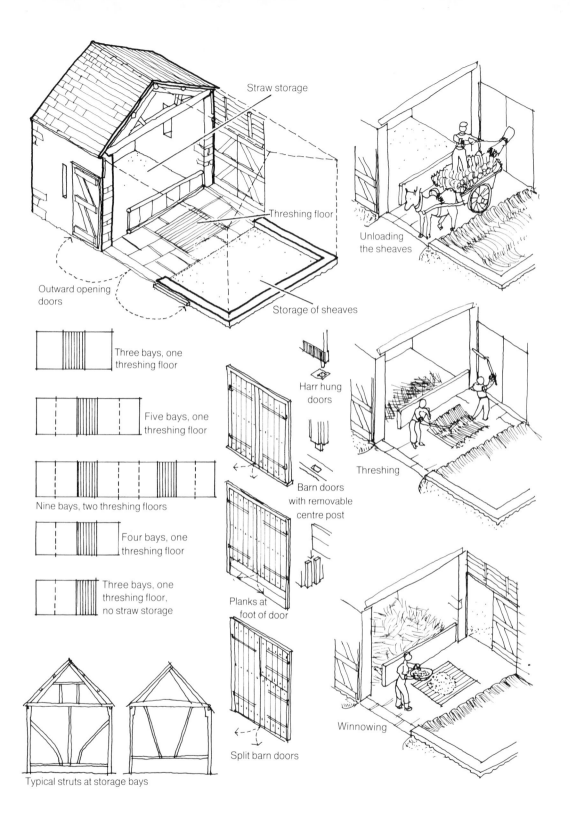

Straw storage

Threshing floor

Outward opening
doors

Storage of sheaves

Unloading
the sheaves

Three bays, one
threshing floor

Five bays, one
threshing floor

Nine bays, two threshing floors

Four bays, one
threshing floor

Three bays, one
threshing floor,
no straw storage

Harr hung
doors

Barn doors
with removable
centre post

Planks at
foot of door

Split barn doors

Typical struts at storage bays

Threshing

Winnowing

ventilation. The space was called the threshing floor. It could be a mat or tarpaulin placed out of doors but was usually a specially prepared floor in the barn. The threshing floor had to be hard enough to withstand the beating of the flail but springy enough to help with its rhythm; it had to be smooth enough to make sure the grains could be swept up without loss; it had to be strong enough to carry loaded carts moving sheaves for storage. Where available, flagstones made up the floor; alternatively there might be a wooden boarded floor; sometimes a removable boarded section was placed on the floor; sometimes there was a boarded section within a flagged, cobbled or brick-paved floor; a well-drained and ventilated sub-floor was recommended. The floor had to be big enough for sheaves to be opened out and teams of threshers to conduct the process.

A tall unobstructed area was required for swinging the flail and even the smallest barns have a height twice that of a man above the threshing floor. The floor was lit by one of the pairs of tall barn doors. The taller the door the greater the penetration of light into the barn and it was important on dark wintry mornings that the threshing team could see that every grain of corn had been dislodged. Usually the doors opened outwards; this ensured that they did not get into the way of the flail. Quite often the doors did not extend as far down as the threshold but left a gap of about 18 inches (457 mm), which was filled by removable boards let into grooves in each door post or the door jambs. These seem to have been intended both to keep flying grains of corn in the barn and to keep hens and chickens outside lest they stray and pick up the precious grain. The framing of the barn doors makes clear that the boards were designed for some purpose and did not simply represent repairs to rotten doors – though there was, of course, every advantage in not having expensive barn doors in contact with damp earth or the manure of the farmyard. The tallest of the barn doors were heavy and not easy to open, especially in wintry weather, and a split or small pass door was often included in their design. A removable centre-post helped secure the doors. Sliding doors did not come into use until about the mid-nineteenth century and were never very popular.

Many barns had equally tall doors at both ends of the threshing floor and it is usually assumed that these were intended to allow carts to be hauled in, unloaded and hauled out again. Certainly the floor was used for unloading; it was quicker to fill a storage bay from a cart on the floor than from outside by way of pitching holes. Certainly where the layout of the farmyard and access roads allowed, it was perfectly reasonable to use one door for access and the other for egress. But the layout did not always so allow. Many a barn had to be built on a slope and level access from the farmyard meant a drop at the opposite doors so that a cart brought in had to be backed out, not too difficult or unfamiliar a manoeuvre for a horse. So the equally tall doors were not primarily intended to suit the carter. Sometimes, and especially in the later and smaller barns, there was a small door opposite the main barn doors. This was not intended, as sometimes suggested, to allow a horse to be unhitched from the cart and led out, but mainly for winnowing.

Often the main barn doors were protected by a canopy, a canopy with cheeks, or by a deep porch. Any protection to the door also protected the threshing floor from driving rain or snow and made sure that the maximum length of floor

15. Barn details

38

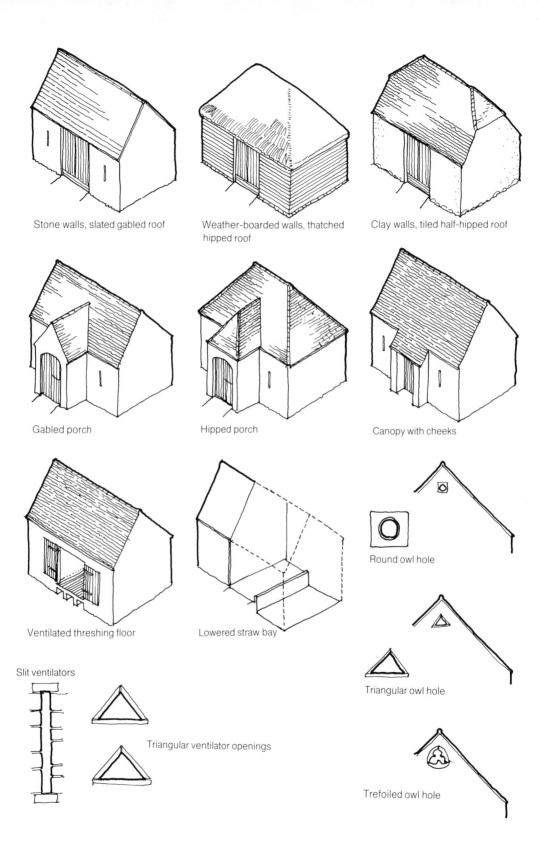

Stone walls, slated gabled roof

Weather-boarded walls, thatched hipped roof

Clay walls, tiled half-hipped roof

Gabled porch

Hipped porch

Canopy with cheeks

Ventilated threshing floor

Lowered straw bay

Round owl hole

Triangular owl hole

Trefoiled owl hole

Slit ventilators

Triangular ventilator openings

39

could be used. The deep porch, and there were several designs, both protected thoroughly the floor and allowed the last cart of the evening to be left under cover to be unloaded the following day.

On each side of the threshing floor were storage bays. At first both were used for sheaves but later one was intended for unthreshed sheaves, the other for threshed straw. When all or most of the crop was to be put into the barn it was important to consolidate the loose sheaves so as to make the best use of the storage capacity and in Suffolk, and probably elsewhere, this was achieved by having a horse or pony tread down the sheaves as they were pitched in. This was known as 'riding the goaf' from the Suffolk term for a storage area or mow. When the back of the unfortunate animal was pressing against the rafters it was lowered by means of a rope and band from one of the roof beams. Although in some timber-framed barns two or three structurally unnecessary posts were

16. Great Barn, Place Farm, Tisbury, Wiltshire Built to serve a grange of the nunnery of Shaftesbury, this is one of the longest barns in England

17. Barn at Stoke-sub-Hamdon, Somerset A conventional three-part hand flail threshing barn with stone walls, slit ventilators, a gabled porch and a thatched roof over stone walls.

included between floor and tie beam to help keep in the sheaves, a well-laid and well-packed mow did not really need such help. Straw, however, was laid more loosely and remained for a shorter time in store. Often there was a low timber partition between the threshing floor and the storage bay; this meant that after threshing the straw had to be lifted and shaken to release any remaining ears of corn before it could be put into store. It also meant that during early summer, when the barn was empty, the straw bay could be used as a pen for sheep waiting to be sheared by men working in the abundant light and pleasant breeze of the threshing floor.

Ventilation to the storage bays was only necessary to a limited extent. Corn was stored dry and needed much less ventilation than hay. In timber-framed barns air could flow through unplastered, wattle panels or between weather boards; in stone barns tall slits or square or triangular holes provided ventilation, while in brick-walled barns gaps were left in the brick bonding to give a diaper, butterfly or honeycomb pattern of ventilation holes. The round opening seen near the gable of a barn wall is the 'owl hole' intended to allow this friend of the farmer to come freely in and out while keeping the mice in check.

So the organisation of the barn: floor, doors, storage bays, height, depth, provision of ventilation can all be seen to relate to the process of threshing by hand flail. Such organisation was also appropriate to the winnowing process.

Once the sheaves had been spread, threshed and the straw lifted out of the way there remained on the floor the grains of corn. They were mixed with chaff, especially the loose cover to the grain itself. In the winnowing process a draught was used to separate the lighter chaff from the heavier grains. Even after threshing had been brought into the barn under cover, winnowing was sometimes still done out of doors. Sacks of grain were taken to a windy hill, emptied on a mat and then with the aid of a light flat basket or a shallow wooden spade girls would toss the grain repeatedly in the wind until all the chaff had been blown away. Open air winnowing, however, is not very satisfactory in this country: it required a dry day, not common in winter time, it allowed no control of the draught so that a sudden gust of wind would blow away grain as well as chaff, and in any case it entailed extra handling and waste of the precious corn. So the winnowing process normally alternated with threshing in the barn on the floor.

Fortunately the requirements for winnowing were indeed similar to those for threshing: a hard clean floor, plenty of light, space and height and a controllable ventilation. For this last the great barn doors came again into use. Even on those few winter days without a breeze some draught could be induced by opening completely one set of doors and partially the opposite set; on very windy days only parts of both sets of doors need be opened. The grain could safely be tossed under cover from basket or by spade till all the chaff was blown away. Eventually it would be riddled to separate the various sizes, put in sacks and taken to the granary but in the meantime it might be stored temporarily in a 'corn-hole', a little area partitioned off the straw bay.

Hand flail threshing was not a pleasant task. From the farmer's point of view it was labour-intensive, as costly as it was inefficient. Conducted day by day in the winter it kept labourers occupied and balanced day-to-day production with day-

18. Barn at Fittleworth, Sussex This small barn has a threshing floor at one end, no straw bay, and storage in a loft. There is a hipped thatched roof and tiled outshuts at each end.

19. Aisled barns, Charleston Manor, Westdean, Sussex Both the barns have the great sweep of roof down to low eaves which is characteristic of aisled barns, but one has an inset door to the threshing floor while the other has a dormer roof forming a porch between the aisles.

to-day needs, but it was difficult to build up a stock of threshed grain and so correspondingly difficult for a farmer to take quick advantage of a sudden market for his grain.

It was estimated at the end of the eighteenth century that a threshing team of a pair of men aided by one or two youths or girls could thresh and winnow up to sixty sheaves of corn in a day, consuming three pints of cider in the process. As yields of corn increased this rate became an increasingly severe brake on the working of the farm. One way of increasing output was to increase the number and size of the threshing floors. In East Anglia it had been the practice from medieval times to provide separate barns or floors for separate crops of wheat or barley; barns with two threshing floors became more common during the eighteenth century. Another way of increasing output was to eliminate the regular – and no doubt welcome – interruption of threshing for winnowing.

There had long been the practice of flapping blankets or sacking to try to add to the draught for winnowing. Early attempts at producing a winnowing machine adopted this principle by attaching blankets to an axle so that when a youth turned a handle the blankets flapped and a draught was created at one end of the floor. This crude device was developed by James Meikle in the 1770s and by the end of the eighteenth century winnowing machines were quite widely used in Scotland, North East England and Yorkshire.

The machine consisted of a hopper into which the grain was fed; a draught was created by wooden paddles or a fan turned through gearing by hand which would blow away the chaff while also separating different weights of grain, so that they could drop through sieves into a series of pockets and so into sacks. The machine was light enough to be moved easily and its simple construction of wooden boards and bars of wrought iron was within the capability of local craftsmen.

Even after the winnowing machine came into use the limitations of hand flail threshing remained a bar to increased farming efficiency and the need for mechanisation was clear. But the manual process had led to the building of what came to be known in other countries as the English Barn: the three-part division of a tall, elongated building into threshing floor with tall barn doors, and flanking storage bays with limited ventilation holes.

Aisled barns

Few would doubt that the finest English barns are the aisled barns. Whether seen from the outside with its roof reaching almost to the ground, tethering the building as if it were a great airship, or seen from inside with its length extending cathedral-like into the distance and its height dimly rising to a web of rafters, the aisled barn impresses as a peculiarly complete building type.

As its name suggests, the aisled barn consists of a central nave rising undisturbed from floor to ridge with lower and narrower aisles at the sides. Unlike cathedrals and most parish churches there is no clerestory, the main roof sweeping down over the aisles to a low eaves. The barn is divided into a number of structural and functional bays, sometimes by stone or brick pillars but mostly by timber posts. A small barn would have three bays, probably the majority have five bays, in each case with a single 'midstrey' or threshing floor. Larger barns of nine or ten bays have two threshing floors as a rule. The largest barns divide each structural bay into two with the aid of an intermediate truss. In the largest aisled barns different storage bays were used for different grain crops.

In the standard aisled barn the nave was flanked by one aisle on each side but in many barns the aisles were carried round each end, creating the impression of a central space with an ambulatory around. This was a common development in Kent, for instance. In a few of the largest examples there were double aisles and in such a barn, when empty, there must indeed have been a forest of timber posts as well as an apparently limitless height to the ridge. In many of the later and smaller examples there was only one aisle.

The width of each aisle depended to some extent on the roof covering. A

thatched or plain tiled roof of steep pitch (50° or so) meant that there was a swift and steep drop between ridge and eaves, whereas a slated or stone-flagged roof of lower pitch (say 35°) allowed a reasonably high eaves line without a ridiculously high ridge. The latter type had a fair ratio between usable storage capacity and the surface area of the external envelope whereas large barns of steep pitch had much wasted volume within the roof space, practically inaccessible before the invention of the mechanical elevator. In either case since the sole or main purpose of the barn was the storage and processing of sheaves, the aisles allowed an increase in storage capacity at the most useful level without a corresponding increase in the length of members needed for roof construction. Nevertheless, the width of aisles in some of the smaller and later barns of very steep roof pitch was so small that the benefits of the design are hard to appreciate.

Generally the aisles were used for storage but in a few cases aisles were fitted out as stalls for cattle. This seems to be a fairly late practice in the southern and eastern counties of England; it probably represents late adaptation of barns. In the northern counties, and especially in Yorkshire, the practice seems to date back at least to the seventeenth century, stalls in the aisles facing on to the nave

20. Aisled barn

44

21. Aisled barn, Wheat Barn, Cressing Temple, Essex This is one of the two great barns at Cressing Temple and is probably of early thirteenth century date. The broad sweeping hipped roof ends in gablets at the ridge.

22. Aisled barn interior, Great Coxwell, Oxfordshire The illustration shows the building in use as a barn; the deep aisles are divided into bays by the aisle posts set on stone pillars.

while doors in the ends of the aisles gave access to manure passages. In these same districts, and in Lancashire, aisles were added to earlier structures, including cruck-framed barns, to meet the demand for accommodation for milk cattle. Although made into aisled barns such structures are not really part of the aisled barn tradition.

The external appearance of an aisled barn with its dominant roof was most affected by the provisions for entrance and how the roof was broken. In order to accommodate full height barn doors it was necessary to break the line of the eaves in some way and there were three main devices for this. The door could be brought forward to the line of the aisle wall with the aid of a huge dormer-like construction, gabled or hipped; this gave space for a longer threshing floor or more space for carts. Alternatively, the door could be brought forward under a hipped or gabled roof to give an even greater extension to the floor as well as a dramatic punctuation to the main roof. Whether hipped or gabled, whether with an even sweep of roof or a slight change of pitch at the junction of nave and aisles, whether with porch or without and whatever the roof or wall covering the aisled barns certainly constitute the most impressive of farm buildings.

The building type is believed to have developed even before the coming of the

23. Aisled barn, East Riddlesden Hall, Yorkshire
This is one of two stone-walled and flagged-roof barns at East Riddlesden Hall. Here the low eaves may be seen as well as the huge and deep porches serving the two threshing floors.

Romans; records also show that quite large examples were in existence in the middle of the twelfth century: the earliest known surviving barn, at Grange Farm, Coggeshall, Essex, dates from only a few years later, while many aisled barns date from the early fourteenth century. Such was the value of this building type and such was the strength of tradition that aisled barns continued to be erected in the eastern and south-eastern counties of England throughout the eighteenth century and even into the early nineteenth.

Most examples may be found to the south and east of a line running from the Wash to Southampton Water and there are concentrations in parts of Suffolk, Essex, eastern Kent and in Wessex. Recent investigation has shown that the larger barns of the Pennines, especially in the Aire and Calder Valleys to the east and the Ribble Valley to the west usually hide aisled construction behind their stone walls. Examples are also known in Leicestershire and further investigation might reveal still more in the eastern midlands.

Superficially the aisled barns may resemble the hall-like barns of North Germany, but whereas German barns often incorporate the farmer's living accommodation and are usually entered through the ends, the English aisled barns are always separate from the farmhouse and always have barn doors in the side walls.

The aisled barn is particularly interesting as a member of the great family of hall-like buildings which dominated architecture in Britain and much of Western Europe for at least seven centuries. The aisled hall was the court or parliamentary building as at Winchester, at Leicester Guildhall and, before it received its present hammer-beam roof, in Westminster Hall itself. The aisled hall is the basis of church planning and a number of timber-framed aisled churches survive, such as Lower Peover in Cheshire. The aisled hall was the form chosen for certain collegiate buildings where members lived communally and St. Mary's Hospital, Chichester is perhaps the best surviving example. The

24. Aisled barn interior, East Riddlesden Hall, Yorkshire The rather low proportions of the barn are different from those of the other aisled barns illustrated. The aisles were fitted formerly with stalls and partitions for cattle.

25. Comparative barn sizes (all are drawn to the same scale)

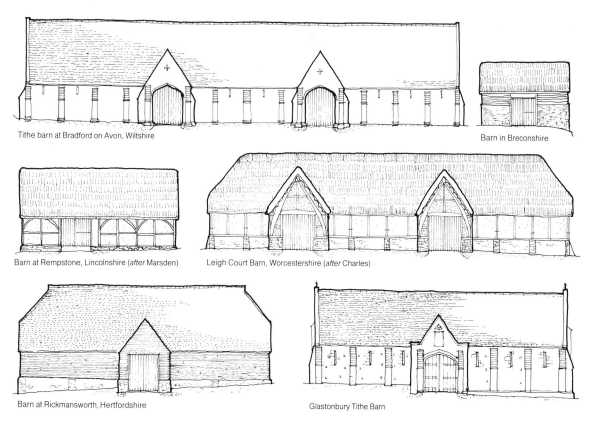

Tithe barn at Bradford on Avon, Wiltshire

Barn in Breconshire

Barn at Rempstone, Lincolnshire (*after* Marsden)

Leigh Court Barn, Worcestershire (*after* Charles)

Barn at Rickmansworth, Hertfordshire

Glastonbury Tithe Barn

timber-framed aisled market hall was a feature of towns in Northern and Central France from the early middle ages to at least the second half of the seventeenth century and although not similarly represented in Britain, the huge timber and iron aisled market halls of nineteenth century Britain show the strength and versatility of the aisled hall tradition.

Barns for machine threshing

Even after the adoption of the winnowing machine the hand flail threshing process remained a serious block on the full use of the increased productivity of arable land. During the later eighteenth century more and better fertilised fields were producing more grain from higher yielding strains of cereal with the aid of more efficient means of cultivation. Unfortunately, the heavy sheaves from burgeoning cornfields could not be used until processed, slowly, by teams of threshers who were increasingly expensive when the farmer was in competition for labour with developing local industries. Naturally, in an inventive age, thoughts were directed to mechanising the threshing process.

Some inventors tried to reproduce the flailing action. Menzies, for instance, attached several flails to an axle turned by a crank and the flails were intended to beat on opened sheaves in direct imitation of the hand process. This and similar efforts failed because any action which produced a strong enough beat tended to

26. Horse-engine house, Trerice, Cornwall This building projects from the barn which contained the threshing machine and has a thin slated roof over a rounded or apsidal wall. Modern hoppers may be seen on each side.

27. Horse-engine house, Washaway, Cornwall This rectangular building is roofed separately from the barn which it serves.

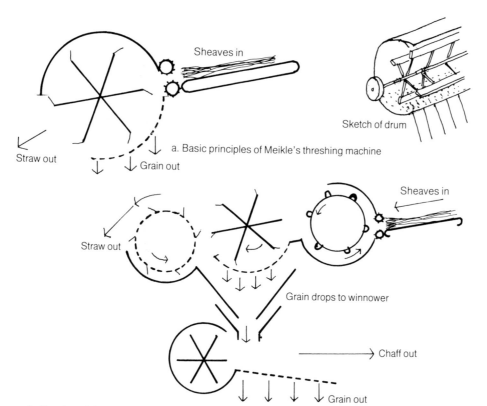

Sheaves in

Sketch of drum

Straw out

Grain out

a. Basic principles of Meikle's threshing machine

Sheaves in

Straw out

Grain drops to winnower

Chaff out

Grain out

b. Developed threshing machine with winnower below

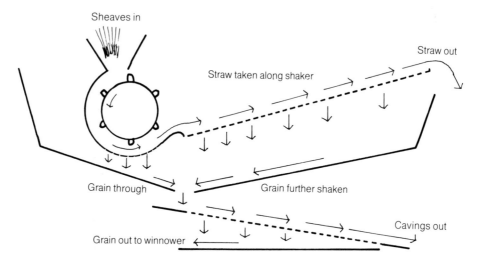

Sheaves in

Straw out

Straw taken along shaker

Grain through

Grain further shaken

Cavings out

Grain out to winnower

c. Machine further developed

28. Threshing machines

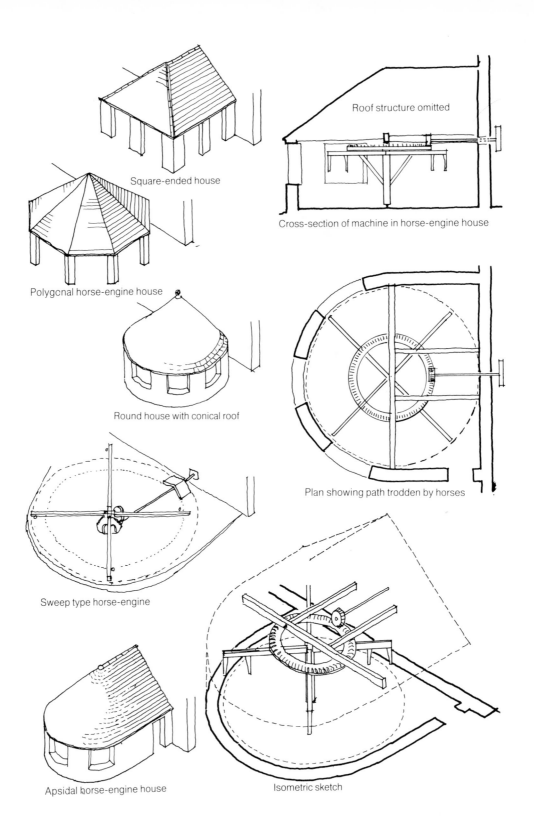

Square-ended house

Polygonal horse-engine house

Round house with conical roof

Sweep type horse-engine

Apsidal horse-engine house

Roof structure omitted

Cross-section of machine in horse-engine house

Plan showing path trodden by horses

Isometric sketch

produce more centrifugal force than the crude leather hinges of the flails could withstand; breakages were frequent and dangerous as broken flails hurtled across the barn. Other inventors attempted to reproduce the chopping action of flax scutching but this was no more successful. The method which ultimately solved the problem was that of rubbing the ears until the grains fell out.

No single person can claim to have invented the process of threshing by rubbing but the idea was successfully developed in Scotland by Andrew Meikle and his son, George, at Haddington, East Lothian, in 1786. Their machine made use of a set of beater arms revolving on an axle and beating the corn so as to rub against a fixed concentric concave screen so that the grains of corn were discharged and the straw could be lifted away. This was a crude but effective process. Improvements were rapidly made, however. First a revolving rake was introduced to order the straw as it was discharged into a series of strands capable of being tied into bundles. Then a shaker was added so that the straw was shaken on its way to discharge, releasing any trapped grains of corn. Threshed and shaken grain was dropped into a winnowing machine which simultaneously blew away the chaff, sorted, dressed and sieved the grain into its various sizes and filled sacks accordingly. Then a mechanical elevator was added to raise the straw into a storage bay or drop into a cart for transport elsewhere. Thus with these few improvements the threshing machine with a small labour force of men, youths and girls could do in hours what had previously taken strong men weeks and even months.

However, a machine such as this required power for its operation. Some of the smaller perfected threshing machines could be operated by hand but with no great saving of labour. Some threshing machines were water-powered, where available water power was cheap and easily controlled, but the machinery was expensive and water was not always available. A few threshing machines were wind-powered: this power source was often advocated in Northumberland, a windy county which had many wind-powered corn grinding mills, but windmills were expensive to build even if cheap to run, farmstead sites were not generally chosen because they were windy in the winter, and at best, wind

29. Horse-engine houses

30. Horse-engine house, Newbiggin, Cumberland
This square building projects from an earlier barn into which the threshing machine had been introduced.

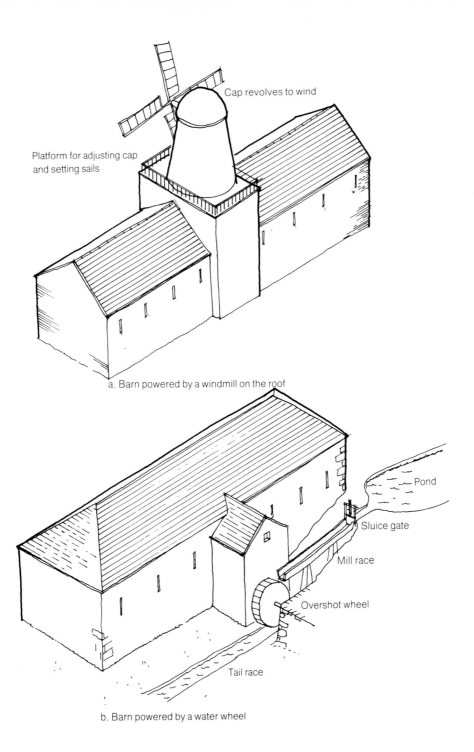

Cap revolves to wind

Platform for adjusting cap
and setting sails

a. Barn powered by a windmill on the roof

Pond

Sluice gate

Mill race

Overshot wheel

Tail race

b. Barn powered by a water wheel

**31. Wind- and water-
powered barns**

power was fitful and unreliable. Steam power was also recommended but was not economical until a cheap and reliable high pressure steam-engine had been perfected, and even then economy depended on a supply of cheap coal. The most frequently used source of power proved to be the horse.

By the late eighteenth century virtually all farms made use of horses for cultivation and as draught animals generally. A farm growing enough cereals to justify a threshing machine would have at least four and as many as a dozen horses, fully occupied in spring and summer, but available for work in the winter months. The horse-engine as a means of harnessing the strength of horses so as to rotate a shaft had long been in use in mines in the form of the 'gin' or 'whim' as well as in building and civil engineering. It is hardly surprising, therefore, that the counties of England and Scotland in which the threshing machine was developed were the very counties in which a suitable method of harnessing power was in use, proven and available. The development of the threshing machine and of the horse-engine took place simultaneously.

There were three types of horse-engine: the overhead type most closely resembling the whim and developed first, the low down or sweep type introduced in about the middle of the nineteenth century, and the treadmill type known in Britain since the middle ages as a power for cranes or lifting buckets in wells, much used in nineteenth century North America but little used here.

In the overhead type of horse-engine two, four or six horses trod a circular path while tethered between wooden forks beneath the ends of long poles or beams; above the intersection of the poles there was a large diameter crown wheel on a vertical axle; a small diameter pinion engaged in the teeth of the crown wheel and converted the slow revolution of the axle to the fast revolution

32. Horse-engine house, Allerford, Somerset
Circular on plan, the stone-walled building has a thatched conical roof.

of a horizontal shaft. This shaft passed into the barn and, with the aid of a belt drive, turned the threshing machine or, indeed, any other piece of barn machinery. The foot of the vertical axle rotated on an iron pin in a socket and at its head a similar pin was caught in a beam forming part of the structure of the roof which covered horses, poles, crown wheel and everything.

Sometimes the horse-engine was contained within the barn but usually it was attached to one long wall of the barn. The horse-engine house might be circular in plan with a conical roof, it might be polygonal but free-standing, polygonal but attached to the barn wall, square with hips back to the barn roof, apsidal with a graceful semi-circular roof sloping back to a ridge or it could be any variation on these shapes. The roof covering varied according to what was commonly used in the locality: probably most are slated but thatch, pantiles and stone flags and tiles have been recorded. The roof was carried on pillars, short stone walls, cast-iron columns or timber posts, always leaving plenty of openings for through ventilation. Horses trod a path which varied between 18 ft. and 30 ft. in diameter (5.5 m to 9.1 m) though between 24 ft. and 26 ft. (7.3 m to 7.9 m) was most common. Generally four horses were needed at a time for threshing, though a big or inefficient machine would require six, while lighter barn machinery could be operated by one or two horses. The work was hard and so at least two teams of horses were needed for a day's threshing. There were ingenious devices for equalising the strain on each horse so that none would be idle and none would over-exhaust himself. Nevertheless, the basic weakness in the design was that the shorter the diameter of the path trodden the less the mechanical advantage gained and the greater the discomfort for horses always pulling to one side, whereas the greater the diameter the greater the difficulty in roofing a structure which also formed part of the machinery.

The sweep type of horse-engine improved conditions. It consisted of cast-iron gearing with one, two or four poles attached leading to a wrought iron shaft with universal jointing. The horses trod a circular path again but pulling the pole by way of traces, as in many farm implements, and along a path of greater diameter. The drive shaft was at ground level but the horses stepped over it using a removable ramped bridge. This type of engine was invented in 1841, displayed at the Great Exhibition of 1851, was relatively cheap to produce, reliable, suitable for small farms and could even be made portable, carried from spot to spot in a cart.

Many horse-engine houses survive, though few with any machinery inside. Few sweep type horse-engines have escaped the scrap dealer but many farms have evidence of their former existence in a paved horse walk or a small opening near the foot of the barn wall through which the drive shaft ran. The distribution of horse-engine houses shows concentrations in the industrial areas of the Central Lowlands of Scotland, Northumberland and Durham, West Cumberland and Cornwall and Devon. They seem to date from the late eighteenth to mid-nineteenth century though very few are accurately datable.

The use of fixed threshing machines, mostly horse-powered, spread from Scotland and the northern counties of England largely according to competition for labour. There was a boom during the Napoleonic War and widespread use in the industrial districts where farmers had a ready market for their produce, including wheat for bread and oats to feed horses, and yet suffered serious local competition for labour. Threshing machines were adopted much more slowly in eastern and south-eastern counties where the bias in mixed farming was certainly towards grain production, but where many hands were needed in spring and summer and so had to be employed on the farm during the winter. Lack of alternative employment in these counties kept wages low and demand for winter work high; the rural riots of the early 1830s were directed especially at such threshing machines as had been installed in those counties.

The advantages claimed for the threshing machine were that it was quicker than hand flail threshing, more economical, produced a better quality grain at a time when the farmer could choose his market, required no casual labour but allowed regular labourers, properly supervised, to work in conditions free from the dust of the threshing floor. On the other hand it was maintained that the machines were expensive in capital and repair costs, were often considered a tenant's item though fixed in the barn, broke the straw, making it useless for thatching, were less thorough in clearing the ears of corn, were dangerous to the operators and, especially, were socially undesirable in taking work away from poor labourers. The horse-engine was considered cruel ('a machine for killing horses'). The balance of advantages favoured use of horse- or water-powered fixed threshing machines in the north and west but delayed their spread into the rest of Britain.

The mixing house barn

The invention of the threshing machine had, in theory, eliminated the need for a barn. Since there was to be no hand flail threshing there was no need for a threshing floor, for the storage bays, for tall barn doors nor for a winnowing door. In existing barns and in new constructions the machine itself occupied one of the storage bays. Yet, at least at first, the introduction of horse-powered or water-powered threshing machines did not completely alter the appearance or layout of the conventional barn. Horse-engine houses or horse walks were added to existing barns, new barns included tall doors to give access to a floor from which sheaves were unloaded for processing in the threshing machine. However, the successful combination of threshing machine and steam-engine meant the transformation and eventually the elimination of the barn.

Three types of steam-engine were used on the farm: fixed engines, portable engines and traction-engines. The fixed engine consisted of a boiler fired by coal and sending smoke up a factory-like chimney stack and steam to a single cylinder engine, placed either horizontally or vertically, with a flywheel and drive to a shaft from which threshing machines and other items of machinery were belt-driven. The portable steam-engine consisted of a firebox and boiler with a horizontal cylinder and flywheel above, but the whole equipment was mounted on wheels and could be drawn from place to place by a team of horses. The traction-engine was like a portable engine but the rear fixed wheels were driven from the engine and the front bogie was controllable from the engineer's platform. Thus the fixed steam-engine could operate a fixed threshing machine on the farm, the portable steam-engine and a wheeled threshing machine could be hauled from farm to farm, while the traction-engine could itself haul a threshing machine from farm to farm and field to field, threshing, winnowing, dressing and bagging the corn in the farmyard or even in the fields.

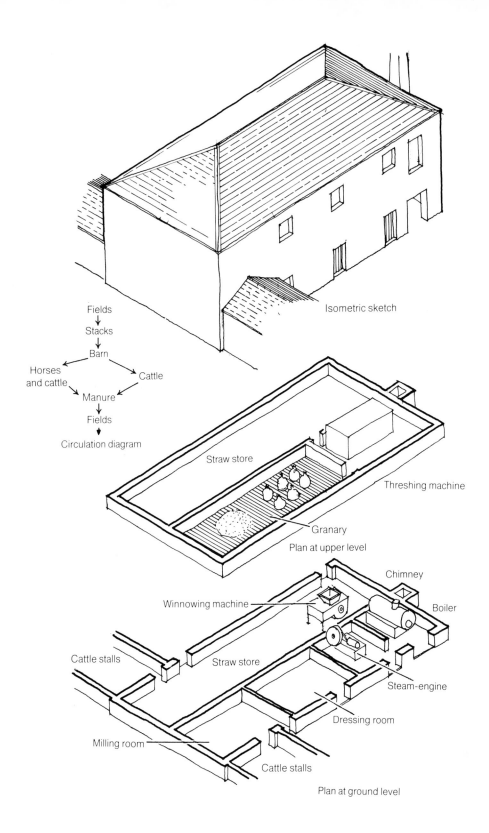

Isometric sketch

Fields
↓
Stacks
↓
Barn
↙ ↘
Horses
and cattle   Cattle
↘ ↙
Manure
↓
Fields
↓
Circulation diagram

Straw store

Threshing machine

Granary

Plan at upper level

Chimney

Winnowing machine

Boiler

Cattle stalls

Straw store

Steam-engine

Dressing room

Milling room

Cattle stalls

Plan at ground level

The fixed steam-engine was only found on the largest farms and then it operated all the machines. On such a farm many stacks of corn would be made on specially prepared stack bases consisting of wooden or cast-iron platforms, raised 18 inches or so above the ground on stone or cast iron staddles shaped to keep the rats away from the corn. Alternatively, and especially where rectangular stacks were traditional, the stack bases consisted of stone platforms, again intended to counter the attentions of rats. When the time came for threshing, each stack in turn had to be broken, loaded on to carts, and taken to the threshing machine. This combination of hard work and double handling did not appeal to the more advanced Victorian farming theorists, and they often

33. Steam-engine and mixing house barns

34. Steam-engine powered farmstead, Gilling, Yorkshire The view shows the engine house and chimney at the back or stackyard side of the long mixing barn range, which in turn served the foldyards beyond.

advocated, and were sometimes able to provide, wheeled stack bases running on railway tracks or tramlines, so that complete stacks could be hauled to be unloaded, even under cover, into the jaws of the threshing machine.

The fixed threshing machine was considered the centre of the well-organised nineteenth century farmstead. From the machine sacks of grain were taken to the granary for storage, for transfer to the mill, for direct sale, or for bruising, kibbling or cracking in the steam-driven mill, before being fed to horses or other animals. Straw was carried up by the steam-driven elevator into straw bays, or a straw barn, from which some of it was taken to the steam-driven chaff cutter which converted it into short pieces for addition to the fodder. The rest of the straw was taken in skips, often running on wheels in a tramway, into the cow-

57

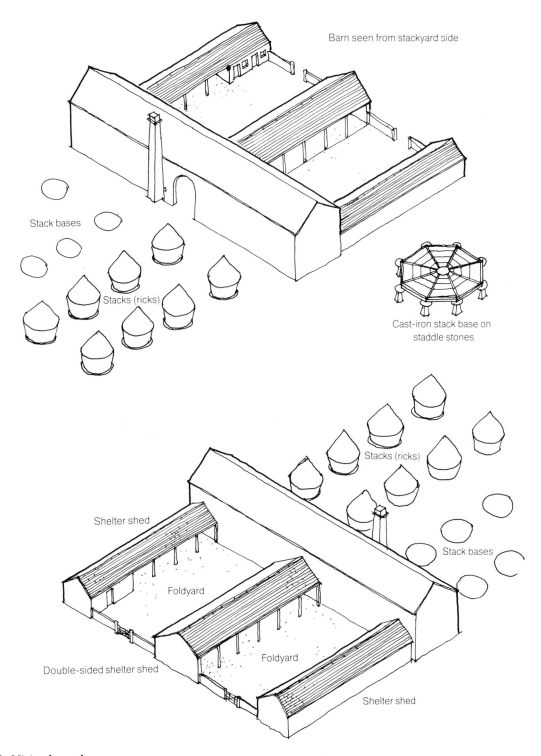

Barn seen from stackyard side

Stack bases

Stacks (ricks)

Cast-iron stack base on
staddle stones

Stacks (ricks)

Stack bases

Shelter shed

Foldyard

Double-sided shelter shed

Foldyard

Shelter shed

**35. Mixing house barn,
stackyards and foldyards**

58

houses for bedding. The threshing machine was placed on an upper floor above the steam-engine and in addition to the chaff cutter the shaft was tapped to drive machinery to slice roots such as turnips, to crush beans or peas, to cut and crush slabs of cattle cake. The waste steam from the engine was used to heat or boil the mixture of hay, chopped straw, bruised oats, sliced roots and oilseed cake when made into a hot meal for the animals.

These various operations depended on the fixed steam-engine and located the engine firmly at the centre of the well-organised farmstead. Eventually more convenient sources of power became available: the gas engine, the oil engine, the petrol engine, the hot air engine and the water engine, all used to varying degrees from the last years of the nineteenth century. Such engines required no preparation, no build-up of steam, no waste at the end of the day and no clearing, riddling and disposal of ash. Nor, indeed, did they entail the fire risk which was always present when a steam-engine was on a farm. However, they could not provide the same sort of flexibility as steam power nor, as long as coal was cheap and of good quality, were they as economical as steam-engines.

The advent of the portable steam-engine and its development into the fully mobile and fully self-contained threshing train provided the farmer with a flexibility in the use of power which he had never before enjoyed. The mobile steam-engine could be used on the farm in farmyard or stackyard. The contractor and his team plus the farmer's own men and help from neighbours ensured that stack after stack of corn could be fed into the threshing machine with its tireless power source and converted into sack after sack of grain and load after load of straw to be stacked again until needed. Alternatively, the corn could be stacked beside the road at the centre of a group of arable fields without haulage to the stackyard, and the mobile threshing train could come and thresh on the spot. With either procedure the task which had taken up every winter's day was now completed in a matter of days if not hours. The main snags occurred on smaller farms and on remote hilly sites. The job of setting up the threshing machine took as long whether the produce of ten or a thousand acres of corn was to be processed; the journey to a large lowland farm beside a good metalled road was infinitely easier than that to a small hill farm accessible only along narrow cart tracks between high stone walls where the traction-engine had frequently to be detached to winch itself and the train into position. So the benefits of the steam-engine were not necessarily available to all farmers; the horse-engine or even the flail had to be called into use until the small petrol-driven tractor and the electric motor became available.

Generally the advent of the steam-engine whether fixed or mobile meant that traditional barns were no longer needed. New farmsteads were built without barns; old farmsteads might retain barns, but for their use as storage for hay or, later, as storage space for sacks of provender or fertiliser. The skyline of the farmstead was changed. Instead of being dominated by the long plateau of the barn roof the silhouette was now broken by the narrow gable of the mixing house and the tall pointer of the chimney stack. In place of the hall-like interior of the barn, the scene of great assemblies for shearing or dancing, there was now only the workshop-like interior of the mixing house with its ranks of cutting, grinding, breaking, stirring machines driven by flapping belts to the steady beat of the steam-engine.

Chapter 3
Accommodation for animals

Introduction

On the typical mixed farm, provision had to be made for cattle (of various sorts), horses, sheep and pigs. The numbers of each category of animal would vary on each farm according to its arable or pastoral emphasis, and, naturally, would depend upon the demand for different varieties of farm produce. As we have seen, until imported or artificial fertilisers became available it was essential to keep animals so that their manure could fertilise the soil. But in their varying degrees, animals provided motive power, consumables such as milk when alive, meat and skins for leather when dead. When we remember that the very horns of cattle made vessels for the medicine used to cure their sick companions, that the hair of the horse's mane provided padding for the collars of his fellows, and that the horn of the ram provided the crook whereby the shepherd caught the ram's progeny, we can begin to appreciate the self-sufficient nature of even quite recent farming.

There was considerable variation in the nature of the accommodation required for different animals at different times. Horses were always considered valuable and delicate and although wild horses could live year after year in the open, horses bred and broken to harness had nearly all to be housed virtually the whole year round. Oxen and milk cows were usually housed for at least part of the year. Young cattle, on the other hand, and cattle fattening for slaughter, were at one time left in the open, but during the phase of high farming they too were kept in some sort of cover. Sheep were nearly always expected to live out of doors and only in certain cases were they housed. Pigs, on the other hand, after centuries of more or less free wandering, grubbing up food in the woods and coppices, when seriously nurtured had to be housed permanently in pigsties and piggeries.

Cow-houses

Cattle were kept on farms as oxen for haulage purposes, as milk cattle to produce milk and so cream and butter and cheese, as store cattle for meat, as breeding cattle for calves, and bulls were also kept. In all these roles they were also needed to consume the produce of the fields and return a proportion as fertiliser. Cattle were kept loose in yards which were open or partially or completely covered; they were kept loose in small cattle boxes; they were kept loose in hammel sheds and small yards or they were kept tied in cow-houses.

The cow-house – known in Lancashire as a shippon, in Yorkshire as a mistal, in Cumbria as a byre – was for the accommodation during the winter of animals too precious or insufficiently hardy to winter in the open. The number of cattle which could be wintered depended entirely on the amount of fodder – hay or

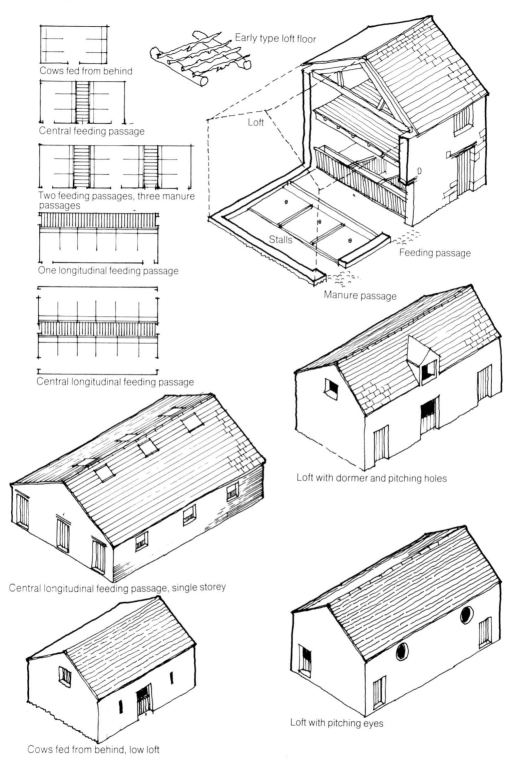

Cows fed from behind

Early type loft floor

Loft

Central feeding passage

Two feeding passages, three manure passages

One longitudinal feeding passage

Central longitudinal feeding passage

Stalls

Feeding passage

Manure passage

Loft with dormer and pitching holes

Central longitudinal feeding passage, single storey

Cows fed from behind, low loft

Loft with pitching eyes

36. Cow-houses

straw principally – which could be amassed and preserved for use during the winter months. While the idea of the autumn massacre of cattle on the farm is no longer accepted, it was not until a combination of root crops, plentiful hay from improved grassland and well-irrigated meadows, and imported cattle cake became available that anything like the present-day number of cattle could be kept on the farm.

Planning of the cow-house depended on numbers of cattle, provision for feeding and 'mucking out', and what provision, if any, was made for the storage of hay. Probably the oldest arrangement, and certainly one with a long history, was that in which the cows were tethered nose on to a wall and fed from behind. An alternative arrangement, and one increasingly followed, was that in which cattle were tethered nose on to a feeding passage running along the length or across the width of the cow-house.

Cattle were arranged in stalls and tied in such a way that they could stand, eat, or lie down without too much discomfort. In the most common arrangement cattle were placed in pairs with a low partition of timber boarding, stone or slate slabs, or, eventually, iron or concrete in between. Sometimes the cattle in each pair were separated by one or two posts so that they could not lie on each other or bump or butt each other. Alternatively, the cattle were tethered singly between narrowly-spaced posts called stanchions. Tethering was usually by a rope arranged to run as a noose up and down a vertical rod attached to the stall division. The details of the tethering varied and some primitive devices avoided the use of metal parts entirely.

Cattle were fed on hay, chopped straw, broken cattle cake etc. and on furze or gorse if nothing else were available. There was usually a hayrack and a manger or loose feeding box in front of each cow.

The floor surface of the cow-house required care in its dimensions, its divisions and its materials. Apart from the feeding passages, two surfaces were important: the sloping surface on which the cow stood or lay and the flat or slightly inclined passageway or drainage channel whereby the cow reached its stall and its dung was deposited, collected and transferred to the midden. The angle of the sloping surface was important: too steep and the cow stood uncomfortably, too shallow and the urine would not drain away. The length was important also: too long and the cow would lie in its own dung, too short and the legs of the cow would be in the drainage channel. The surface material was important: the stall had to be hardwearing but not unpleasant under the straw bedding. The manure passage had to be easily cleared with the aid of a shovel or 'group' so that the muck could be deposited in a midden in the yard, or, through pitching holes, could be piled near the opposite side of the cow-house for immediate carting to the fields. The agricultural writers of the nineteenth century recommended various dimensions such as fourteen feet (4.3 m) from wall to wall for a single row of cows and one manure passage, and thirty feet (9.1 m) from wall to wall for two rows, central feeding passage and two flanking manure passages, for instance. But these dimensions were established after a period of improved breeding. In looking at older cow-houses we must remember that at one time full-grown cattle were much smaller than the ones to which we are now accustomed.

Until well into the nineteenth century, the cow-house was a low, dank, ill-lit

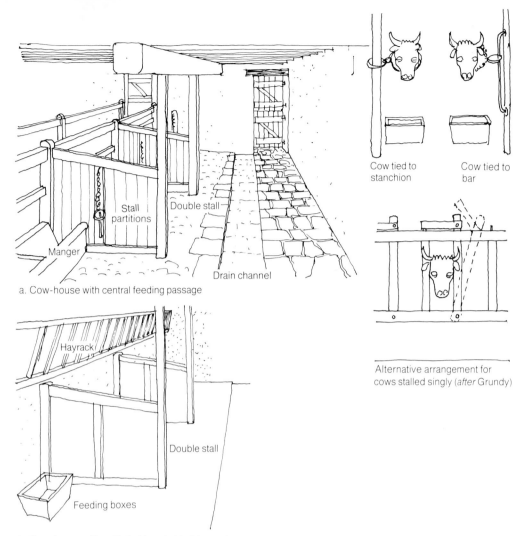

a. Cow-house with central feeding passage

Cow tied to stanchion

Cow tied to bar

Alternative arrangement for cows stalled singly (*after* Grundy)

b. Cow-house with cattle fed from behind, hayrack, loose feeding boxes

37. Cow-house details

and ill-ventilated place. Usually there were no windows at all, light and ventilation coming from the open top half of a split door and from slit ventilator openings, where provided. In stone-walled cow-houses, especially, a warm comfortable fug developed during the winter months, and in the warmth beasts continued to thrive on limited and indifferent fodder. The cow-house was a much warmer place than the farmhouse kitchen, let alone the dairy, and this must have relieved the monotony and drudgery of milking during the winter.

The cow-house was low in height and snug in atmosphere because hay was stored in the loft above. Some of the earlier and more primitive lofts survive in which a boarded loft floor is lacking; instead there are main beams across the building and branches of trees or poles cut from hedgerows spanning between the beams; these crude joists supported a bed of bracken or, in the better-favoured farms, a mat of woven straw rope; on this the hay was piled. Openings between the beams, or specially placed hatchways, gave ladder access and

38. Cow-house at Castell-y-garn, Newport, Pembrokeshire The single door gives access to a cow-house in which the cattle are tethered facing each end wall; there are no ventilation or window openings.

allowed the cowman to draw and drop the daily supply of hay. In some instances, especially in the Pennine areas, the hay loft extended downwards to ground level at one or both ends of the cow-house in what was called a 'sink mow'. Hatches in the walls then allowed hay to be dragged out by the armful and the level of hay in the mow dropped correspondingly each winter's day. This arrangement approached the ideal of the 'self-feeding barn' which American farmers cherished, though it is doubtful if any herd of cows was ever allowed to eat entirely at will in such a cow-house.

The amount of hay stored in the loft related to the productivity of the meadows or of the fields growing grass as part of a rotation of crops. Early cow-houses, and those on the less well-favoured hill farms had very low hay lofts, virtually confined to the roof space; later cow-houses, and especially those on the more productive lowland farms, had tall hay lofts and sometimes the loft was taller than the cow-house below. Hay in the loft was well protected and, with some attention to ventilation, could be kept in good condition, but it had to be pitched into the loft and packed into the eaves and between the roof trusses with some labour. Pitching holes (i.e. square window openings with a shutter instead of glazing) were provided in the cow-house gable or under half-hipped thatched roofs and by way of a dormer in the front wall facing the farmyard. In brick-walled cow-houses, especially as found in the midland counties, circular pitching eyes were used (the circle approximating to the shape of a truss of hay on a pitchfork). Tall openings with double-width doors were provided in the later cow-houses which had very large lofts, and even then it was sometimes necessary to include mechanical devices to allow trusses of hay to be drawn from the pitching holes into the depth of the loft.

Agricultural theorists from the mid-nineteenth century onwards deplored the use of the hay loft. They believed that light and ventilation were good for cattle and rather than have the cows wallowing in the dusty fug of the old cow-house they should be more hygienically accommodated in airy cow-houses which were lit by roof-lights as well as by windows in the walls. By the late nineteenth century, in any case, hay, though still important, was only part of the winter diet, and hay was now kept in thatched stacks or in specially designed hay barns.

Throughout the late eighteenth and the nineteenth centuries there were experiments directed towards finding the most efficient means of housing cattle and their fodder. Much labour was spent in tending cattle, especially during the winter months, and as labour became more expensive, labour-saving became more worthwhile. Time spent in feeding could be reduced when all cattle faced a single long feeding passage and so long narrow cow-houses were built. To reduce time spent in 'mucking out', and to ensure that all the valuable solid and liquid manure was preserved, experiments were made with two-level cow-houses, the cattle standing on a slatted floor at the upper level and the manure accumulating on the lower level until needed on the fields. The Harleian System in the Glasgow area is the best-known of these experiments. Savings from such economies were only justified on the largest farms and until late in the nineteenth century the traditional cow-house, with its characteristic arrangement of three or five doors denoting cattle ranged across a lofted building, continued to be built and used.

One further aspect of housing tethered cattle deserves mention. The rapidly increasing demand for milk and dairy products during the Industrial Revolution coincided with developments in storage and processing of cereals which, as we

39. Cow-house interior, Strata Florida, Cardiganshire This has been constructed or adapted to provide double stalls with feeding passage running along the length of the building. The cow-house is open to the roof, there being no loft above.

have seen, diminished the importance of the barn. So cattle stalls were inserted into or added to barns which were filled with hay rather than sheaves; suitably wide aisles could be adapted in this way and unaisled barns, such as those built with cruck trusses, had cow-housing added to make rather incongruous and awkwardly constructed aisles. On some of the small hill farms new cow-houses were added to existing buildings, sometimes as a lean-to taking up a barn wall but with no intercommunication, sometimes as an extension, lengthening a farmhouse and creating a longhouse type out of what had previously been a separate farmhouse.

Farmyards and foldyards

Whatever the size of the farm and whatever the type of farming we expect to find a farmyard, a place defined in some way, however loosely, by the buildings of the farmstead – a place which acts as a circulation area giving access to the various buildings and providing links between them, a place which contains in winter the ever-growing mountain of manure, its bacteria working up a heat turning organic matter into fertiliser. On many farms and in many parts of the country the farmyard was also the foldyard and as such played an important part in the accommodation of cattle.

From the mid-eighteenth century onwards the rapidly increasing number of cattle tethered in the cow-house was matched by the number increasing, at least as rapidly, of cattle who spent the whole year in the open. These included the young heifers not yet old enough to calve and the young bullocks not yet old enough to be fattened for slaughter. In most parts of the country there was no

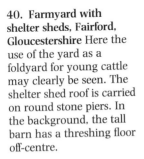

40. Farmyard with shelter sheds, Fairford, Gloucestershire Here the use of the yard as a foldyard for young cattle may clearly be seen. The shelter shed roof is carried on round stone piers. In the background, the tall barn has a threshing floor off-centre.

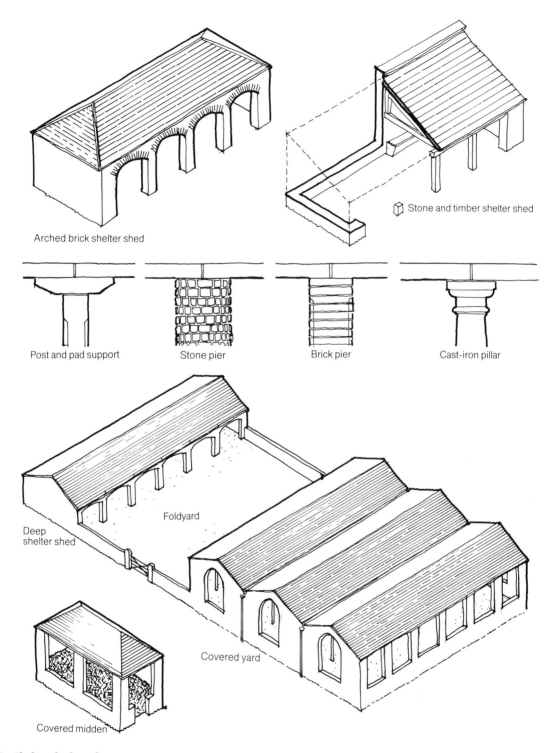

Arched brick shelter shed

Stone and timber shelter shed

Post and pad support

Stone pier

Brick pier

Cast-iron pillar

Deep shelter shed

Foldyard

Covered yard

Covered midden

41. Shelter sheds and foldyards

need to house them and they soon became too numerous for housing to be economical. At the same time they could not be left in the fields during the winter: there was no grass to nibble and it was good neither for soil nor beast to have hooves treading away at cold wet land. The answer was to fold such cattle in the farmyard. Here they were sheltered from the winds, food and water could be made easily accessible, and here, under supervision and controlled conditions, they could continue their most important task – the conversion of crops into meat and manure.

The smaller farms had a single farmyard doubling as a foldyard, but on the larger farms there might be several foldyards, allocated to different groups or ages of cattle. In the planned farmsteads beloved of enthusiastic landowners and built from designs circulated and published by architects, land agents and farmers from the early eighteenth century onwards the foldyard was a major item. It seems likely that the freedom in design of foldyards helped to encourage the move of farmsteads from cramped sites in the villages to more open sites among the fields which took place especially during the late eighteenth and the nineteenth centuries.

The foldyard was a cheap but very satisfactory type of accommodation for young cattle, especially in the eastern half of Britain where winter rainfall was relatively low, where straw was produced in increasing quantities, and where manure was needed for more and more intensively cultivated fields.

Shelter shed

It was recommended by agricultural writers that the foldyard should face south to benefit from the sun and should be protected on the north by the barn against the coldest winds. On at least one side the foldyard was also further protected by a shelter shed.

This simple piece of the farmstead plant was a long single-storey building, open-fronted, but with solid end walls and one solid side wall. The roof was carried above the open front on piers of stone or brick or columns of timber or cast-iron. Within the shelter shed were troughs to serve as mangers and racks to hold the hay; these were usually ranged along the rear wall but sometimes they were set in short runs at right angles to the wall. There were no stall divisions and there was no need for any means of tying the cattle. The shed provided shelter from the worst of the weather and a place in which cattle could be fed, thus reducing waste, maintaining their quality during bad weather, spreading out the cattle during feeding time and to some small extent reducing the opportunities for strong cattle to bully and steal food from the weak.

Where there were several foldyards in order to separate various categories of loose cattle, keeping numbers within reasonable control and helping with supervision, then, of course, there would usually be several shelter sheds. Sometimes adjacent yards or large single yards had a double-sided shelter shed. In some farmsteads the shelter shed was designed as part of a larger building – under a loft, for instance, alongside a stable, or adjacent to the straw barn of a machine-powered mixing house.

Neither shelter sheds nor foldyards were confined always to the main farmstead. During the mid-nineteenth century especially, shelter sheds were added to field barns to make outfarms or satellites to the main farmstead.

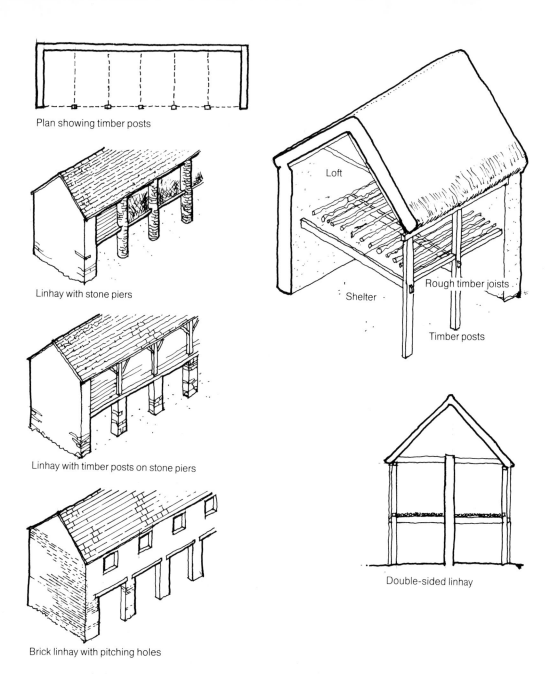

Plan showing timber posts

Linhay with stone piers

Linhay with timber posts on stone piers

Brick linhay with pitching holes

Loft

Shelter

Rough timber joists

Timber posts

Double-sided linhay

Linhays

An interesting variation on the shelter shed was developed in south-western England and called there the linhay. This consisted of a shelter shed beneath an open-fronted hay loft. Like a shelter shed a linhay usually had one solid wall and two solid end walls, the front consisting of piers of stone or even cob, or of wooden posts. Part way up the piers may be seen the beams or arches which carried the loft floor. This was sometimes boarded but often it consisted of rough boughs or hedgerow poles closely spaced to carry the hay. Sometimes there was

42. Linhays

69

43 Shelter shed at Allerford, Somerset The thatched roof is carried on round stone piers.

a gap near the back wall through which the hay could be pulled into the hayrack for the cattle. The hay loft above the shelter shed had a completely open front or a few rails and studs to keep in the hay. The roof was sometimes of double pitch but perhaps more often of single pitch, and the term 'linhay' is used generally in reference to the vernacular architecture of the south-western counties to mean a lean-to or 'catslide' roof.

Linhays are very common in Cornwall and Devon but they are also found in South Wales and occasionally in the West Midlands. It is rather surprising that such a neat, economical and labour-saving design for the accommodation both of loose cattle and their fodder was not more widely used.

Covered yards

However useful rain might be in circulating the fertilising agents in the fields it is the enemy of successful manure-making in the farmyard. Rain washes away the liquid manure and its valuable salts, and although it might wash this liquid by way of drains into a slurry or liquid manure tank serving as a reservoir until the liquid could be pumped into wheeled tanks and so taken for spraying on the fields, the more diluted the liquid manure the bigger the necessary reservoir and the more wasteful the carting. There was every advantage in protecting the manure from rainfall.

At the very least the rain falling on the roofs of buildings surrounding the yard could be led away, and at a time when gutters, downspouts and surface water drains generally were not provided for humble buildings they were advocated for the buildings around the foldyard. Another way of guarding against waste or dilution was to provide a covered midden in the farmyard: a high containing wall kept the manure concentrated, a simple roof on piers protected it, and a gap in the wall allowed the midden to be cleared in springtime. Such covered middens were quite popular during the second half of the nineteenth century, but they fell out of favour as they required plenty of labour to fill and empty them, were relatively less important as imported or artificial manures became available, and in any case did little to preserve the muck being trodden into manure by the cattle in a foldyard. Few covered middens are now to be seen; they have been abandoned, demolished or converted to other uses.

Yet another way of dealing with the problem of soggy dung and diluted manure was to cover the whole yard. A roof gave further protection to the cattle (though some writers thought this made them less hardy) but, more importantly, rainwater falling on to the roof could be directed to a surface water disposal system and away from the manure. The main advantage claimed for a covered yard was that it avoided dilution and waste, but it was also claimed to minimise the waste of straw. This was not a particularly important point when straw was plentiful, but it became so as the balance of mixed farming swung away from arable towards pastoral during the last two decades of the nineteenth century and economy in straw did become important.

Covered yards were regarded as novelties in the 1860s but came into increasing use later in that century and remained popular at least until the time of the First World War. A large area of roof, however, had to be carried on piers and columns and even when corrugated iron replaced slates and tiles, the first cost was quite high and maintenance of the essential guttering and drainage system was another expensive item which eventually diminished the popularity of the covered yard.

Hammels, bull pens, cattle boxes and loose boxes

Between the two extremes of cow-house and foldyard there was the loose box in its various forms. Whereas cattle were completely restricted in the cow-house and completely free in the foldyard they were partly free and partly confined in the loose box and its variations.

A *hammel* consisted of a room big enough to contain two, three or even four cattle, depending on their age and size, but without stalls or any provision for tethering, and off which opened a small yard of approximately equal size to the room. In the enclosed part of the hammel the cattle could shelter, sleep on straw bedding and tread manure; in the small yard the cattle could be fed and could exercise at will. The hammel was especially popular in Scotland in the early years of the nineteenth century, and some of the largest Scottish farms of this time had row upon row of hammels, but the plan was also used to a limited extent in England – in Northumberland and Staffordshire, for instance. The hammel gave more freedom to cattle than stalls, was reputed to keep them cleaner, and made them better able to tread dung into manure; at the same time it allowed easier segregation of sick or troublesome cattle than in the foldyard, as well as better protection from the weather. It probably required more labour than the foldyard but less than the cow-house.

The *bull pen* was a special version of the hammel. There was a house for the bull and a walled yard, bigger and more secure than the yard of the hammel.

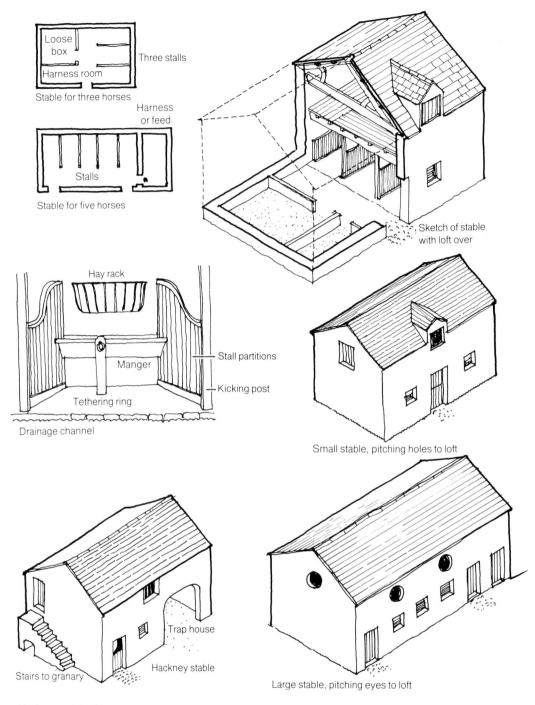

Loose box

Harness room

Three stalls

Stable for three horses

Harness or feed

Stalls

Stable for five horses

Sketch of stable with loft over

Hay rack

Stall partitions

Manger

Kicking post

Tethering ring

Drainage channel

Small stable, pitching holes to loft

Trap house

Stairs to granary

Hackney stable

Hackney stable with granary over

Large stable, pitching eyes to loft

44. Stables

Cattle boxes were cubicles, within a building, containing a single ox or two smaller cattle. A row of cattle boxes achieved something of the economy in space of the cow-house while allowing something of the freedom of the hammel. However, cattle boxes required much labour in 'mucking out' and were relatively expensive in terms of cattle housed. It is hardly surprising that cattle boxes were more often recommended in books than used in practice.

The ordinary *loose box* is found on practically every farm. A loose box consists of a room or compartment with a door, also a window as a rule, and no other formal provision. Loose boxes could be used for single cows when sick or calving; they could serve as a hospital ward for a sick or foaling mare; they could accommodate little groups of bullocks or heifers in bad weather or when the full provision of foldyard and shelter shed was not available. Many hill farming districts have legends about young cattle kept all winter in the loose box until they could scarcely squeeze between manure level and doorhead in springtime. A unit as versatile as the loose box was essential to the satisfactory running of a farmstead full of specialist buildings and spaces designed for specific purposes.

Stables

The horse was the prince of animals; providing mobility for the knight in war and for the gentleman in peace, it was for many centuries spared the labours of the farm. The ox was the draught animal. The horse was expensive to buy or rear, temperamental in use, tending to fragility in health, expensive to feed and requiring a special diet, including oats. The horse also required special grooming and was almost worthless when dead. The ox, on the other hand, was correspondingly cheap to rear, stolid and docile in the yoke, hardy, not prone to sickness, easy to accommodate, undemanding in food and providing valuable meat and skin when a useful life came to an end. But the ox was slow and far from versatile, and so from the seventeenth century onwards was gradually replaced by the horse. Sometimes horses were added to an ox team. Sometimes horses were used for work in which speed and adaptability was important while oxen remained in use for straightforward ploughing. By the end of the eighteenth century, however, the horse had replaced the ox on nearly every farm and the various implements whether plough or rake, seed drill or harrow, as well as every cart and wagon were drawn by horses. At the same time the introduction of the horse-powered threshing machine ensured that the team needed for spring, summer and autumn work did not remain idle during the winter.

Horses for farm work were bred to be powerful and dependable, and breeds such as the Clydesdale and the Suffolk Punch were widely used during the late eighteenth and nineteenth centuries. More elegant and spirited animals were kept as riding horses or for hackney use to draw the coach or trap. Farm horses and hackney horses had separate stables on the farm.

Although in some of the drier counties horses wintered in yards with shelter sheds, in most of Britain a stable was considered necessary for the comfort, health, safety and security of the horses. Spacious stalls and loose boxes provided for comfort and safety, a tall floor to ceiling height and controllable ventilation provided for health, while the proverbial stable door, when locked,

45. Stables at Stoke-sub-Hamdon, Somerset Two adjacent stables are set under the one thatched roof. The loft is served by the two 'eyebrow' dormers around the pitching holes.

provided security. In contrast to the cramped cow-houses of the eighteenth and early nineteenth centuries the stable was spacious, airy and well-lit. Like the cow-house, the stable was usually placed beneath a hay loft but sometimes a granary or even domestic accommodation was placed over the stable. As with cow-houses, later stables were single-storey, open to the roof and had roof-lights and ventilators as well as windows in the walls. This arrangement was considered more hygienic and avoided tainting the fodder with the smells of the horses.

The stall in the stable was quite different from that in the cow-house. Usually each horse was given an individual stall, though in Scotland the earliest stables had no stall partitions while after about 1770 it was quite a common practice to place in double stalls horses which worked with each other. Common dimensions for individual stalls included nine or ten feet (2.7 m or 3 m) between head and foot and six feet (1.8 m) between stall partitions, giving enough space for the horse to lie down or to stand up when being fed or groomed. The stall partition (called a travis in Scotland) was strong and heavily boarded, stout at the rear to absorb kicks, tall at the head to prevent the horses biting each other and reinforced in the middle where the horses were liable to lean. At the head there was a manger into which the oats were poured, and, above, a rack of wood or wrought iron for hay. There was rarely a feeding passage in a stable; almost invariably horses were fed from behind. Often there was a hatch above each rack whereby hay could be drawn from the hay loft. Where there was a granary above the stable there were associated tales of grooms who bored holes in the ceiling so that favourite horses could be given extra rations of oats. As in the cow-house the design of the floor was important. It had to be impermeable but comfortable and giving a firm grip to the feet, sloping very little from front to rear but easily cleaned into a drainage channel. Special pavior bricks were developed for use in stable floors.

46. Stable, Cathedine, Breconshire A very characteristic detached stable; there is a tall and wide doorway set between generous windows with a loft served by a tall dormer window above.

As in the cow-house there were various recesses and cubby-holes in stone or brick walls and here a candle, a horn for medicine, or curry combs could be kept; but unlike the cow-house the stable presented the special problem of accommodating the harness. Although it was considered harmful to both the metal and leather parts of the harness for it to be hung in the stable, such an arrangement was convenient and separate harness rooms are not often found near stables for working horses.

Pigsties and piggeries

Pigs have always played an important part in the rural domestic economy though until recently a much less important part in agricultural economy. Able to produce a large litter, requiring little attention, rapidly putting on weight, able to live and even flourish on food scorned by other animals, the pig could serve both as gleaner and scavenger.

During medieval times pigs ran in herds nuzzling among the woods and coppices for mast, acorns etc. in the charge of the swineherd. Later, and especially from the mid-eighteenth century onwards, under pressure from the enclosure of common land the main home for the pigs shifted to the farmyard. By this time, selective breeding was changing the pig from a hairy muscular animal into the pink, bristly, even downy animal to which we are accustomed, vulnerable to cold weather, vulnerable to draughts and best able to produce a litter, suckle the piglets and put on weight in the snug comfort of a sty. The standard pigsty developed as a low loose box, big enough to accommodate one or two pigs and with a small exercise yard with some trough and feeding arrangement.

The loose box was usually single-storey but sometimes had a poultry loft above. It was low, barely big enough for a man to stand in unless bent over, had a door, a ventilation slit or sometimes a window opening. The yard was slightly

75

bigger, had a tall and stout wall, and a feeding trough. The pig swill, based on meal and sliced root crops, was prepared in the boiler, domestic or farmyard, and to protect the lad or lass in charge of the pigs from an over-enthusiastic rush at feeding time there was usually a chute outside whereby the swill could be poured into the feeding trough inside with a stout baffle separating the two. The ordinary family farm would have a pair of pigsties built together, larger farms had correspondingly more, maybe as many as eight in a row.

There was one interesting variation in the conventional pigsty which is seen here and there, especially in the southern half of Wales. This is the circular pigsty with the conical roof. In this design the sty is circular on plan and stone walls rise until they are gentle corbelled (or projected) inwards to meet at the apex of the solid stone roof. This type of construction is found quite widely in Mediterranean countries and is represented, for instance, in the 'trulli' of Southern Italy and most famously in the 'Treasury of Atreus' at Mycenae in Greece, but rarely in Britain. The technique requires no timber either for centering or for roof construction, requires no tools or any real mason's skill, makes use of flat stones wherever they may be quarried or picked from the fields. There seems no reason why it should be connected with pigsties except that they were small buildings, had to be quite strongly built and needed only a short roof span.

At the opposite end of the building scale were the piggeries, sometimes called 'Scandinavian Piggeries' recommended by some of the nineteenth century agricultural writers. Such a piggery consisted of a series of walled boxes for the pigs with a feeding passage and sometimes a manure passage, all under cover, and in a building looking like a single-storey cow-house. There was usually a boiler or feed-preparation room at one end of the building and sometimes the piggery was heated, on the grounds that it was cheaper to make the pigs comfortable with coal than with corn.

In areas of less severe climate, small herds of pigs, especially young pigs maturing and fattening, were kept in yards with a shelter shed. This was an economical arrangement in terms of the conversion of straw and muck into

47. Stables interior, Beamish Open Air Museum, Co. Durham The separate stalls have high and stout timber partitions. On the right are two chests for oats.

48. Farmyard with pigsties, Llandegman, Breconshire Farmyard with its central midden. There is a shelter shed on the right and single-storey pigsties at the rear.

49. Pigsties, Beamish Open Air Museum, Co. Durham There are two pigsties, each one having a tilted stone serving trough, and there is a poultry loft above.

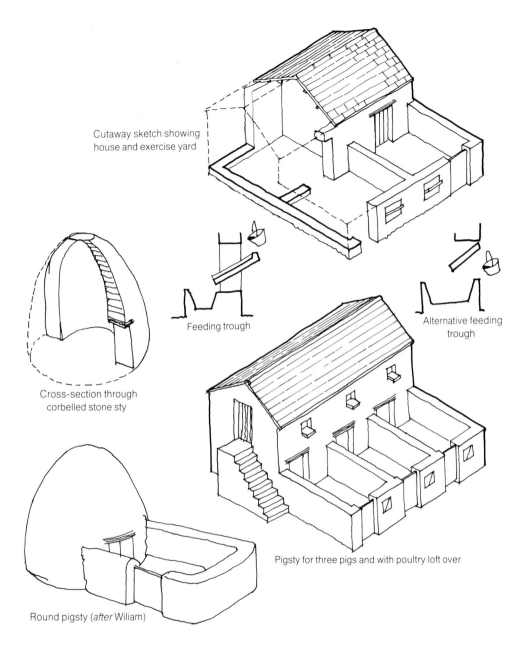

Cutaway sketch showing house and exercise yard

Cross-section through corbelled stone sty

Feeding trough

Alternative feeding trough

Pigsty for three pigs and with poultry loft over

Round pigsty (*after* Wiliam)

manure. Where the climate was more severe, pigs were sometimes kept in loose boxes, again with straw litter to make into manure.

Very few domestic pigs are kept nowadays and then in loose boxes rather than in pigsties. Commercial pig-rearing is done on a large scale and then in scientifically designed buildings. The traditional pigsty is the least adaptable and probably the most vulnerable of all the buildings of the farmstead.

As transport improvements succeeded one another during the eighteenth century there was a developing trade in smoke-cured bacon and ham. In addition to the pigs kept for domestic consumption some were kept for slaughter,

50. Pigsties

salting, smoking and then transport on the turnpike roads or the canals and coastal shipping routes for consumption in London and the other fast-growing cities. Where the farmhouses retained hearths on which wood or peat was burned then the chimney or lath and plaster chimney hood served for smoking the side of bacon. Otherwise a special smoke-house might be provided and these may occasionaly be found complete with beams and pegs for hanging the meat and some sort of hearth and smoke hood for guiding the curing smoke. In Scotland some of the larger farmers distributed salted bacon sides for curing in the smoke hoods of cottages where peat was still burnt.

Hog-houses for sheep

Generally sheep were assumed to require no covered accommodation. On lowland farms they were folded behind hurdles in relatively sheltered fields, on highland farms they were brought down from the most exposed pastures in the worst of the weather. However, there may be found in Cumbria and some other hilly districts a type of building intended for the accommodation of sheep and called the hog-house. In this sense a hog is a yearling sheep enduring its first winter. Such young sheep were not yet fully hardy and in the winter months were brought down to the more sheltered fields for exercise and to graze as best they could but also to be fed on hay.

The hog-house consisted of a low-ceilinged loose box at one level and a hay loft above. The building was usually placed against a slope so that the hay loft might be filled from the upper level while the hogs reached their shelter from a lower level. Day by day the hay was taken from the loft to be fed to the sheep and, in the worst of the weather, they could take shelter in the lower level under the heavily insulating hay loft.

A hog-house was rather like a field barn in use and appearance, but the low height of four or five feet (1.2 m or 1.5 m) indicated design for sheep rather than cattle.

51. *Top* **Pigsty, Manaton, Devon** These massive granite stones form the feeding entrance to this ancient pigsty.

53. *Centre* **Pigsty, Manaton, Devon** Interior of pigsty showing the granite feeding trough.

53. *Right* **Boar Pen, Manaton, Devon** The boar was kept apart from the other pigs in this special pen.

54. *Above* **Hog-house, near Helton, Westmorland** Set across the slope, there is access to the upper level of the building through the gable and the sheep may reach the lower level at the corner. The foot of an upper cruck blade projects slightly from the side of the building.

55. *Right* **Linhay, Leinthall Starkes, Herefordshire** Set within a range of farm buildings, the linhay has the characteristic shelter shed below and hay storage above.

Chapter 4

Accommodation for birds

Introduction

A moment's thought will make one appreciate what an important part is played by birds, their flesh and their eggs, in our present-day diet even though we are now able to tap the animal and vegetable produce of the whole world. How much more significant, therefore, were birds wild and tame in the much more restricted diet of the days when food meant home-grown food. Right until the time that mosses and marshes were drained, moors enclosed and woods felled, the landlord legally and the tenant or cottager rather less legally could snare or trap or shoot at birds enough to vary his diet. At the same time some birds were domesticated and their production controlled. The most important in terms of farm buildings were doves or pigeons and rather more domesticated, but less tied to buildings, were poultry, ducks and geese.

56. Dovecot, Avebury Wiltshire This is a small but typical dovecot, circular on plan, with a conical stone-tiled roof and a glover or cupola at the top for access by the birds.

Dovecots

The dovecot (also known as a pigeon house or culvery) was a familiar feature on certain farmyards from the middle ages to the eighteenth century; many survive but few remain in use. Pigeons provided fresh food in winter: the old birds at the

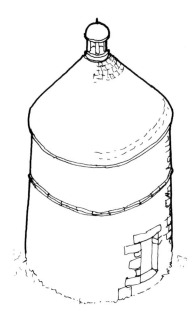

Round stone dovecot with conical roof

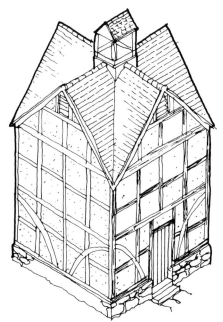

Square timber dovecot with gabled roof

Square clay dovecot with tiled half-hipped roof

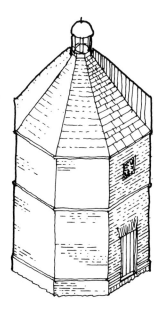

Octagonal brick dovecot with hipped roof

57. Dovecots

81

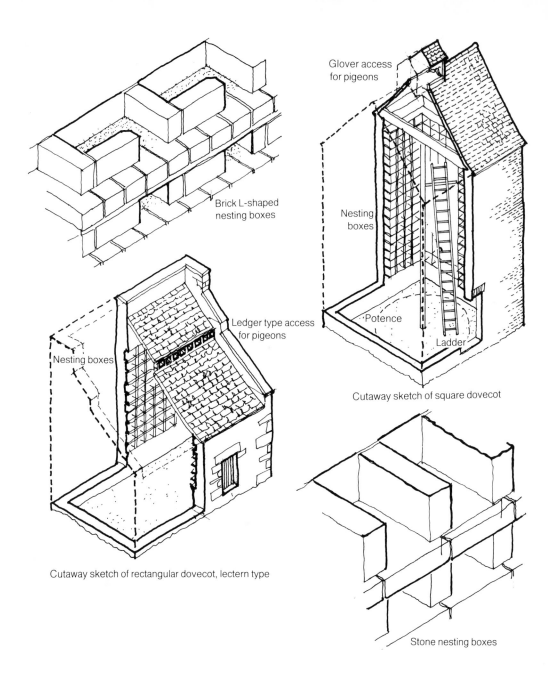

Glover access
for pigeons

Brick L-shaped
nesting boxes

Nesting
boxes

Nesting boxes

Ledger type access
for pigeons

Potence

Ladder

Cutaway sketch of square dovecot

Cutaway sketch of rectangular dovecot, lectern type

Stone nesting boxes

58. Dovecot details turn of the year and the young birds in spring relieved a diet of dried or salted meat. At all times pigeon eggs were regarded as a tasty addition to the diet. Needing little labour the care of pigeons was popular among those entitled to have them. The pigeon manure was regarded as especially powerful and was welcome as a leavening to the midden. The right to maintain a dovecot was restricted to privileged landlords, monasteries and parochial clergy. Even so it was estimated that by the seventeenth century there were 26,000 dovecots in

England alone. After root crops came into cultivation in the late seventeenth century and the eighteenth century and as yields of hay meadows increased it was easier to keep animals over the winter. As a result, given an animal was due to be slaughtered, it was no longer necessary to choose November rather than February for slaughter, so fresh meat could be available at any time and therefore pigeon meat was no longer so important. At the same time tenant farmers were no more inclined than they had ever been to have their fields stripped by the landlord's pigeons. An Act of 1761/2 allowed any landowner or freeholder to build a dovecot on his own land and any tenant to build one with his landlord's permission. Few new conventional dovecots were built after this date though some more decorative structures were built, especially on model farms, and

59. Dovecot at Luntley Court, Herefordshire The square, timber-framed dovecot has four gables and a miniature gabled roof to the glover at the top.

60. Dovecot at Walkern, Hertfordshire This octagonal brick dovecot has quite elegant patterning and decoration of the brickwork and a delightfully shaped glover at the apex of the tiled roof.

more generally dovecots were incorporated in other buildings.

There were three main designs for dovecots: the beehive, the lectern and the tower. The beehive dovecot consisted of a cylindrical stone tower tapering towards an opening for pigeon access, this opening often being crowned by a largely decorative cupola. The beehive dovecots are found especially in the Scottish Lowlands and tend to be sixteenth century or earlier in date. The lectern type was a square or double square on plan with a single pitch roof and access openings in the roof, as a sort of unglazed clerestory, or immediately underneath the eaves. These tend to be of late sixteenth century and seventeenth century date and are fairly common in Scotland but rare even in northern England. The third type, by far the most common, was basically a tower with a pitched roof. The tower might be square, circular, octagonal or in some other way polygonal on plan; it might have a conical roof, a many-hipped roof or be gabled on two or four sides. Access for pigeons was by dormer in the roof or by a glover (i.e. a covered opening) at the apex of the roof, or by openings near the top of the walls.

61. Dovecot roof construction, Minster Lovell, Oxfordshire The difficult problem facing the carpenter providing a conical roof is illustrated here.

Construction might be of timber-frame, brick, stone, flint, cobble or even clay, with roofs of thatch, slate, plain tiles or stone tiles. Some such towers are supposed to be medieval but most range in date from the late seventeenth to the early nineteenth century.

The dovecots were lined with nesting boxes. These were made of stone, brick, tile or timber partitions. The simplest consisted of open-fronted boxes about eight inches (203 mm) wide and tall and fifteen inches (380 mm) deep, but some craftsmen, more in England than Scotland, favoured a larger and shallower box with an eight inch square (203 mm square) opening and a more completely enclosed nesting space. Access was also needed for collecting eggs and mucking out so dovecot doorways were low in order to discourage birds from flying out. There was usually a step down to floor level to allow for some accumulation of manure. Nesting boxes were reached simply by a ladder or, more commonly, the dovecot was equipped with a potence, a tall revolving axle with a projecting arm against which the ladder could rest (rather as the old

62. Dovecot interior, Minster Lovell, Oxfordshire The illustration clearly shows the pattern of openings to the nesting boxes (which widen out inside the wall) and the ledges on which the birds alight.

lamplighter used to lean his ladder against an arm at the top of the lamp-post). Occasionally, wide fixed ladders projected from the axle so that two people could collect eggs at the same time. Difficulties in access limited the dimensions and proportions of dovecots. Most accessible were those circular or octagonal on plan; square dovecots required the egg collector to stretch into the corners; rectangular dovecots had to be double square or rather less on plan to allow two potences to be used. The number of nesting boxes in a typical dovecot was enormous. Most had between 500 and 700 double-sized boxes and around 1200 nests, but examples with as many as 2000 boxes have been recorded in Scotland. Taking an average of 700 boxes in, say, 30,000 dovecots then there must have been, in the early eighteenth century, something like 2,000,000 pigeons in purpose-built accommodaton alone.

At this time, distribution of free-standing dovecots was widespread. They have been studied with particular reference to the Lothians of Scotland, to the Cotswolds, and to Worcestershire, a county especially rich in surviving dovecots, most of those built between 1500 and 1700 being half-timbered.

Later dovecots, incorporated in buildings, show as grouped openings usually in gable walls. In one type each opening had a short projecting platform from which the pigeons went into nesting boxes in a little garret underneath the gable, which was reached from inside the barn, granary or hay loft. In the other type, the opening was as before but each served a single nesting box and eggs were removed from outside. By this time, pigeon manure was no longer considered an important product.

63. Dovecot at Outlaw, Angus A very large and capacious rectangular dovecot of a type not uncommon in Scotland; the single-pitch roof is set between crow-stepped gables.

Poultry houses

Only the privileged could keep pigeons but anyone could keep hens and the farmer's wife and the cottager's wife alike took advantage of the right. Until very recently the hens, along with the ducks, geese and turkeys comprised a separate little farming enterprise run by the farmer's wife independent of the larger operation, contributing to the family diet but also giving the wife a slight degree of independence by way of poultry and egg sales.

On the farm, until this century, poultry ran freely during the day, picking up scraps from the farmyard. It was in the interests of the farmer's wife that laying hens were encouraged to lay in special boxes safe from predators, rather than in cosy but hidden and vulnerable spots among the hedgerows, and that all hens could be shut in at night secure against foxes or other animal or human dangers. An upper level poultry house or loft met both requirements: warm lined nesting boxes were there for the laying hens, roosting bars were available for night-time use and small lockable doors secured the poultry. Mostly the poultry house was placed over the pigsty and a stepped or ramped access leading to a little slot served the hens and an access door the egg collector.

Other birds generally had no special provision. Turkeys are delicate and easily frightened and so they might be given the run of a loose box. Ducks had the pond. Geese are too fearsome to require either care or protection but a little hutch was sometimes provided at the foot of the steps leading to the granary so that geese could give warning, Roman style, of any marauders.

Chapter 5

Granaries and other provision for the storage and conversion of crops

Introduction

We have seen that the barn was a place in which crops were temporarily stored before and after processing, and that cow-houses, stables and linhays included space for the storage of the hay which was to be fed to the animals. There were, however, special building types designed exclusively for the storage of crops of various kinds and in various states or for their conversion into something else. Principal among these building types are granaries, kilns for corn-drying, hop-roasting or barley-malting (all of which had attendant buildings) as well as hay barns and similar structures which served only to shelter harvested crops.

Granaries

As long as the yield of grain crops was low there was no need for a special building in which to store the grain. The largest monastic granges or manorial farms might have a space to serve as a granary, but on the ordinary farm the precious grain was kept in the house for the short time between threshing and consumption or sale at the market, or the rather longer time until a significant proportion of the crop was used as seed in the following season. As yields increased a separate place was needed in which the grain could be stored in secure, dry and well-ventilated conditions until sold, consumed or sown. A granary gave the farmer a chance to hold his crop until the best market opportunity was presented rather than having to release his crop as soon as it was available at whatever the price.

Although grain had been stored in pits in the ground in dry countries – and even in Britain during the Roman period – it was always understood that grain was best stored where surfaces were dry, where ventilation was good, where conditions were clean and where some protection from vermin could be expected. With these requirements the granary raised above the ground was devised as a building type.

There were four main types of granary: the free-standing granary, the granary raised over a cartshed, the granary raised over a stable and the granary combined with food preparation.

The typical free-standing granary was a square, single-storey box raised on nine or more staddle stones. Usually such a granary was timber-framed, the interior was plastered or timber-lined, the exterior was weather-boarded, tile or slate hung, or there were panels of brick-nogging. The roof might be thatched but more often was covered with slates, stone tiles, plain tiles or pantiles. Within, the floor was divided by low timber partitions between which the grain could be stored loose or kept in sacks or chests (grain stored loose was less easy to steal than that in sacks!). The boarded floor was tightly tongued together both to

keep in the grain and to keep out the rats and mice. Generally, wall, floor and roof materials were tight-fitting, clean and secure. A single carefully made and hung door opened, when unlocked, on to a removable platform leading to steps. The platform, as defensive as a drawbridge, allowed for a gap between steps and door which vermin could not jump. Grain is quite heavy and so the floorboards and their joists were carried on stout beams with short spans between the supporting staddle stones. Each of these was made normally of stone, sometimes of cob, and, in later instances, of cast-iron. In every case the smooth curving pillar, giving no grip to the feet of mice or rats, was surmounted by a projecting cap which could not be climbed. Thus the raised free-standing granary kept the grain sweet, with the aid of ventilation to all surfaces, and secure with the aid of anti-vermin design.

Not all free-standing granaries were exactly of this design; some of the larger ones were rectangular and had twice the floor space of the standard square plan; some of the largest rectangular granaries were two storeys in height, and with central door and flanking windows or ventilation panels at two levels, gave a curiously domestic appearance. Nor were all such granaries of timber-frame construction; some were of brick (or a soft stone such as clunch on a brick base) and then piers and arches served to provide ventilation and protection in place of the staddle stones and timber beams.

The free-standing granary may most commonly be seen in the south-eastern half of England. Examples abound in such counties as Cambridgeshire, Berkshire, Sussex and Dorset but use extended into Devon and Cornwall also.

Probably the most common arrangement was the granary over a cartshed. That very increase in productivity which had given rise to the need for a granary had been achieved, at least partly, with the aid of implements which had to be protected from rain, or wood which needed protection from the sun. The need for a granary to be raised from the ground complemented the need for a cartshed to be an open-fronted roofed structure. Thus the standard cartshed/granary had a completely enclosed granary floor raised over an open-fronted cartshed of two, three or more bays. Again, the granary was plastered or lined with match

64. Granary at Rhoscarrock, Cornwall
This is a timber-framed, slate-hung granary set on sixteen staddle stones.

65. Granaries

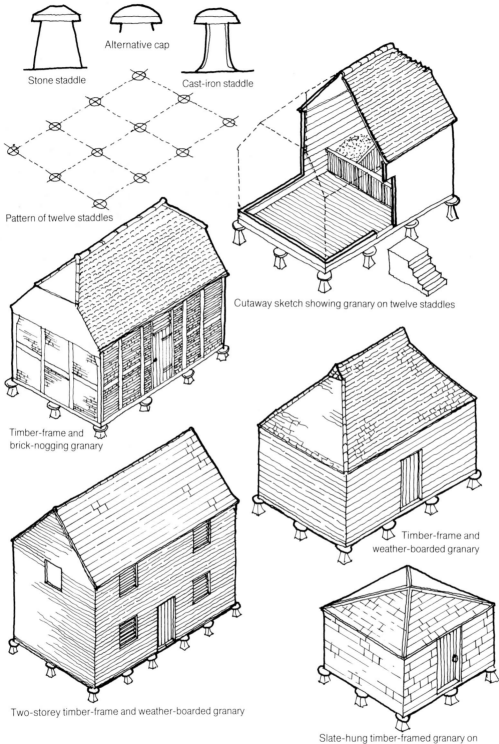

Alternative cap

Stone staddle

Cast-iron staddle

Pattern of twelve staddles

Cutaway sketch showing granary on twelve staddles

Timber-frame and
brick-nogging granary

Timber-frame and
weather-boarded granary

Two-storey timber-frame and weather-boarded granary

Slate-hung timber-framed granary on
nine staddles

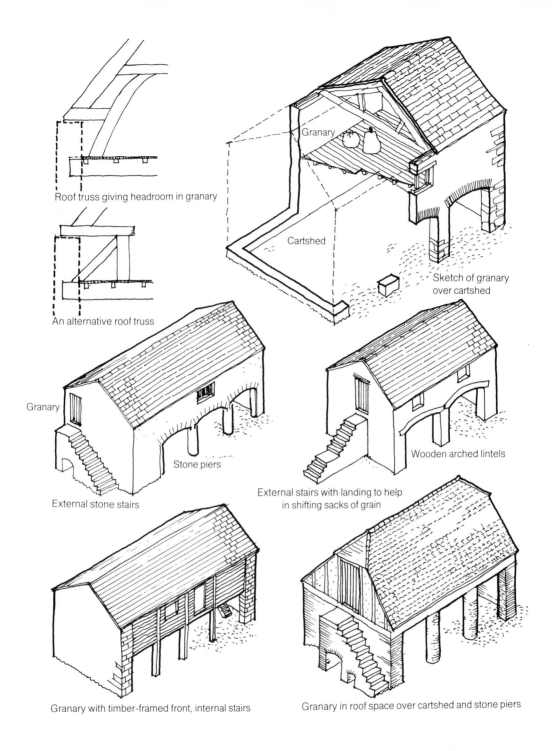

Roof truss giving headroom in granary

An alternative roof truss

Granary

Cartshed

Sketch of granary over cartshed

Granary

Stone piers

External stone stairs

Wooden arched lintels

External stairs with landing to help in shifting sacks of grain

Granary with timber-framed front, internal stairs

Granary in roof space over cartshed and stone piers

66. Granary/cartsheds

boarding, and often had a plastered ceiling. The close-boarded floor and joists were carried on heavy beams dividing the cartshed into bays and these in turn were carried on piers of stone or brick or on columns of timber or iron. Access to the granary was usually by an external staircase but might be, alternatively, by an internal staircase opening off one of the bays of the cartshed.

Sometimes one bay of the cartshed was made open at both ends so that a cart could be drawn through. Where there was such an arrangement then a trap door in the floor of the granary allowed sacks to be dropped directly into carts for transport off the farm. Sometimes, on very large farms, the granary section of the building had two storeys: either two complete storeys or, more commonly, a storey in the roof space. With such an arrangement the farmer had great flexibility in storage according to the sequence of good years and bad years, according to variations in the proportion of land under the plough, and according to cyclical fluctuations in the market, keeping some grain back for one or two seasons.

In the third arrangement the granary was placed over the stable rather than the cartshed. This was convenient in that the horses were great consumers of the oats kept in the granary but it was a less than satisfactory arrangement in that there was no free ventilation of the granary floor: in fact grain could be tainted by the smell and sweat rising from the stable.

The fourth type of granary was that which formed part of the total food preparation and distribution unit found as part of the mixing house barn. Then the granary was as likely to accommodate imported grain, including maize, as that grown on the farm; temporary storage in the granary was as likely to lead to some food processing machinery as straight to the mangers of the animals.

Provision of granaries, then, began with estates such as monastic granges in which crops were grown and collected for sale or transport to monastery, cathedral or college. The great age of granary provision was from the later eighteenth century to the late nineteenth. Separate free-standing granaries are characteristic of southern and eastern lowland areas and found in south-

67. Granary near Hertford, Hertfordshire A very large two-storey granary, the domestic appearance is belied by the outward opening hoist door on the upper floor. The removable steps serving the door may be seen leaning against the wall.

68. Granary/cartshed, Strata Florida, Cardiganshire This typical structure has an external flight of steps giving access to the granary set over its open-fronted cartshed.

69. Granary interior, Fenni Fach, Breconshire Set over a cartshed, the rather low granary, accommodated mainly in the roof space, has 'post and pad' detail at the foot of the principal rafters to replace the tie beam which would otherwise interrupt the floor space.

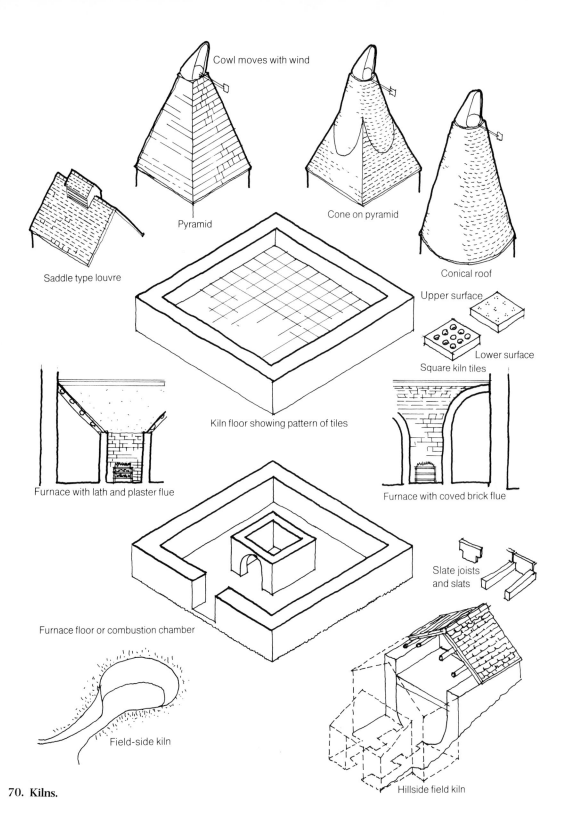

Cowl moves with wind

Pyramid

Cone on pyramid

Conical roof

Saddle type louvre

Upper surface

Lower surface

Square kiln tiles

Kiln floor showing pattern of tiles

Furnace with lath and plaster flue

Furnace with coved brick flue

Slate joists and slats

Furnace floor or combustion chamber

Field-side kiln

Hillside field kiln

70. Kilns.

western counties, whereas granaries over cartsheds are almost universal in the midlands, northern and north-eastern counties of England and in most of Wales and Scotland.

Corn-drying kilns

Visitors to some of the colder and damper parts of Britain are often surprised to discover that grain crops were once grown in districts where neither the climate nor the soil would appear to be particularly suitable. The younger farmers in these districts are often equally surprised to discover that their predecessors had farmed in such an apparently odd fashion. Yet as part of the mixed-farming economy grain had to be grown both for food and for straw and during periods of farming expansion the area devoted to such mixed farming was pressed further and further up the slopes and into the damper parts of northern and western counties. In such districts and where long-term changes in climate were turning a once-favoured district into one less favourable to cereal cultivation occasional bad harvests left corn unripened. And in those areas where the corn growing season was generally short it was also necessary, either regularly or occasionally, to have the corn dried. This could be done in a temporary or permanent kiln.

The temporary kiln was a saucer-shaped stone-lined sinking in a bank within a field, usually in a corner and usually near a stream. Hot air from a wood or peat fire was drawn through the kiln until the sheaves were dry; the adjacent stream was needed in case the grain caught fire. The remains of these kilns in distant fields or near the farmyard may be found with careful investigation though somewhat similar structures were used for other purposes – burning potash for instance – and even when the kiln has disappeared its memory may remain in a field name such as 'Kiln Field' (or in Welsh 'Cae yr Odyn').

Small permanent kilns were sometimes included in the farmhouse. A little chamber was built alongside the hearth or fireplace and small quantities of grain were heated day by day. Once again it is important to note that such domestic kilns might equally have been designed for another purpose, such as the roasting of a little barley to make malt.

The complete purpose-built permanent kiln consisted of a low firing chamber with a coved funnel directing heat from a charcoal or peat fire through a platform on which damp grain was spread in layers three or four inches (75 mm ot 100 mm) thick. This platform ultimately consisted of square perforated tiles carried on iron joists, but until such refinements were available the grain was spread on a horse hair blanket carried on slats of stone or slate, which in turn were carried on stone beams. The platform was contained within a roofed structure ventilated to help induce a draught and carry away the moisture-laden air and tall enough to allow a man to turn and shovel the grain. Some-times the kiln was placed against a bank so that the drying floor could be tended from an upper level and the furnace from a lower. Sometimes, and examples have been recorded especially from northern Scotland, the kiln was a square or circular appendage to a barn.

Corn-drying kilns have been in use at least since Norman times and excavations in surviving and deserted villages have indicated the use of kilns in highland areas and especially in upland villages vulnerable to cold, damp conditions. During the eighteenth and nineteenth centuries, however, it became customary to add kilns to the water-powered corn mills found in such districts. This was more economical than the farmyard kiln for it allowed continuous rather than intermittent use. The farmyard kiln passed out of use and few are now to be seen.

Oast houses or hop-drying kilns

Hops were introduced to this country as a crop possibly as early as the late fourteenth century or the fifteenth century and their cultivation developed during the sixteenth century, first in Kent and Sussex and later in Herefordshire. The plant was trained to climb up strings set between poles in well-sheltered fields and the cones of the flowers of the female climbing plants formed the basis for the dried hops needed for brewing bitter beer. Hops were gathered in September and dried during the winter. Natural drying proved unsatisfactory for substantial quantities of hops and artificial drying in a hop kiln was recommended as early as 1574.

A complete oast house or hop house consists of space for the storage of green hops, a kiln, and a place for the storage for about ten days of dried hops before they are packed tightly into long sacks called 'pockets'. The storage space is located on an upper level in a small rectangular building while the kiln is a tall building on a square or circular plan. The kiln itself consists of three parts: the combustion chamber at ground level, the drying floor above, and the working area and cowl on top. Early combustion chambers generally consisted of a brick fireplace or furnace with a lath and plaster flue widening out like an inverted pyramid to meet the underside of the drying floor. From about 1780 onwards the lath and plaster flue was superseded by a brick continuously coved flue,

71. Oast house near Cranbrook, Kent Two oast houses, one square the other circular on plan, are set one at each end of the storage building.

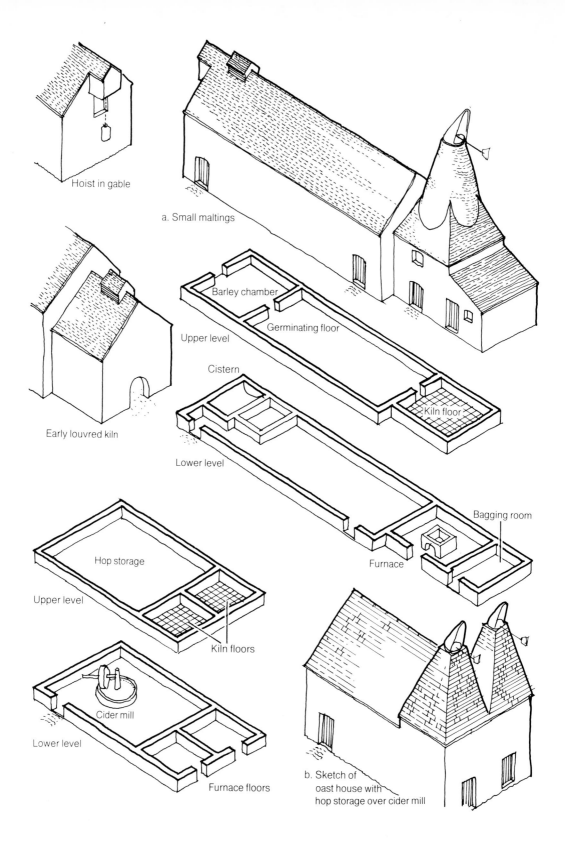

Hoist in gable

a. Small maltings

Early louvred kiln

Barley chamber

Germinating floor

Upper level

Cistern

Kiln floor

Lower level

Bagging room

Furnace

Hop storage

Upper level

Kiln floors

Cider mill

Lower level

Furnace floors

b. Sketch of
oast house with
hop storage over cider mill

72. Oast houses and maltings.

73. Oast houses, Stoke Lacey, Herefordshire Two circular oast houses, each with a conical roof, are placed behind the storage building. In the background one may see a dovecot formed in the gable of a farm building.

again widening from furnace to drying floor. The fuel was charcoal or anthracite. Alternatively, the flue gases from a coal fire were led through brick or metal flues to a chimney, heating the hop-drying floor on the way. The drying floor consisted of a horse-hair cloth stretched on slats or joists. Hops were spread on to the cloth to a depth of as much as twelve inches (305 mm) and were regularly turned by the labourer using a specially shaped shovel. The time on the drying floor would vary from as little as six to as many as twenty hours, but eleven hours was normal. In some cases sulphur was burned to help give the dried hops a yellow colour. A full-height working area was needed. Above, there was in earlier hop houses a roof with a saddle-type louvre to let out the moist air, but later the roof was converted into a tapered flue which met a cowl automatically set against the wind by means of a horizontal vane. This sort of cowl was an invention of the 1790s.

The hop-drying kiln may be incorporated in a building or may be a separate part of the farmstead complex and may have either a square or circular base. The oldest and smallest kilns are incorporated in buildings; older separate kilns tend to be square on plan; from about 1835 round kilns were introduced because it was thought that they were more economical to construct and produced the best draught; from about 1875 there was a return to square kiln shapes as it was realised that the round shape made little difference. In the kilns of the late nineteenth and early twentieth centuries the square shape allowed for the horse hair blanket to be mounted on rollers and turned to help agitate the hops and speed up their drying.

Most hop kilns are found in Kent and Sussex. Cultivation started there and the great city of London provided a market for hops in its many breweries and a labour supply at the time of the hop harvest from its streets. It is hardly surprising, therefore, that the typical rural scene in those counties is always assumed to include an oast house. The building type is also found in Herefordshire and Worcestershire, since the counties had, by 1880, come to supply a quarter of the hop harvest. There the structures are often combined, rather incongruously, with provision for cider-making, the kiln being at the end of a building whose upper level stored green hops and whose lower level housed the cider mill. In both hop-growing districts the kilns are often found in pairs, one storage wing serving two kilns. The great majority of these buildings are of nineteenth century date and have brick walls, whether round or square on plan.

74. Maltings, Burwell, Cambridgeshire The long, multi-storey storage and germinating levels end in a kiln whose conical roof has lost its cowl.

Maltings

Malting kilns were designed to help the process of converting barley into malt by means of controlled germination. The malt was used especially in the brewing of beer, but was also part of general human diet.

First the barley was taken from store and soaked in water for about two days,

then it was spread quite thinly on a large floor where, with the aid of some limited circulation of air, the barley began to germinate. The process continued for eight to ten days and then was arrested when the germinating barley was dried in a kiln. The dry malt was then bagged, stored on the farm for gradual sale, or sent away for use or sale. The malting season was traditionally from September to April.

The small, farm-sized maltings consisted of a two-storey building with the kiln at one end. Sacks of grain were hoisted into the barley chamber, unbagged and then dropped into the cistern of water for steeping. The damp barley or 'couch' was then lifted to the long low working floor where it was spread and turned and moved during the germination period. The working floor was usually of timber but plaster floors, made out of a gypsum mixture, may sometimes be seen, as may floors of tile. Gradually the grain was moved to the kiln floor and in due time it was spread out to be dried. Like corn-drying and hop-roasting kilns the malting kiln consisted of three parts: the furnace level, the drying floor and the flue with its revolving cowl. The methods of heating were similar to those used in other kilns but the drying floor was covered either with wire gauze or with square, perforated kiln tiles. Until the late nineteenth century, malt was taxed and so a maltings operated rather like a bonded store; the couch was measured by the excise men so that the due tax could be assessed and the windows or ventilation openings were barred so that the malt could not be stolen.

Few farmyard maltings are to be seen nowadays. They were superseded during the nineteenth century by maltings on a much larger scale, located rather as industrial buildings beside canals or railways from which deliveries of barley could be converted in huge quantities, or located with breweries so that the malt could be fed directly into the vats for brewing. However, on some farmsteads, especially in eastern counties, the characteristic kiln and its cowl betrays the maltings as a building of the farmstead.

Hay barns

As long as meadows were relatively unproductive, the limited amount of precious hay available could be kept in the lofts over cow-house and stable. When the floating of water meadows and, later, the introduction of grass for haymaking as part of a crop rotation increased the production of hay, the surplus could be stored in larger lofts, in haystacks, or in both. Hay is easily spoiled through exposure to rain and damp hay is prone to spontaneous combustion. Even if a haystack is thatched the hay is open to the weather as soon as the stack is broken for consumption to begin. Storage is ordered best if the hay can be protected by means of a roof, but well ventilated through the absence of walls. There developed, therefore, especially in the wetter regions, a special building type, the hay barn, different from the barn proper in that it was intended for the storage of hay rather than the conversion of cereal crops. There were two main types: those with a fixed roof (sometimes called Dutch Barns) and those with an adjustable roof (sometimes called French Barns).

Since a hay barn consisted effectively of a roof for maximum protection and open sides for maximum ventilation, a common type had a slated roof on trusses supported by piers of brick or stone or by columns of timber or iron. Often the end walls were solid, but perforated by ventilation slits or of honeycombed brickwork. In Snowdonia the hay barns had roofs supported on massive orthostats of slate. In Cheshire the roof was sometimes supported by pointed arches in brickwork giving an oddly medieval impression.

The hay barn with an adjustable roof consisted of a roof framed up to form a rigid lid which could be raised and lowered on four poles, one at each corner. Obviously the advantage of this type of hay barn was that the hay stack was well covered whatever its height, but the disadvantage was that the ropes and pulleys needed to adjust the roof were easily jammed or broken.

Hay barns were recommended at the end of the eighteenth century and the early years of the nineteenth century but were not often built as permanent structures after the 1860s, appearing rather as temporary constructions of telegraph poles and corrugated iron. Hay barns may be found anywhere in the midland and northern counties of England but are most common in Cheshire and South Lancashire, in Derbyshire and in North Wales.

75. Hay barn near Maentwrog, Merionethshire The roof is carried on great orthostats of slate.

76. Haybarn, Adlington, Cheshire The slated roof is carried by brick piers and the brick end wall has a gay pattern of ventilation holes.

77. Haybarns.

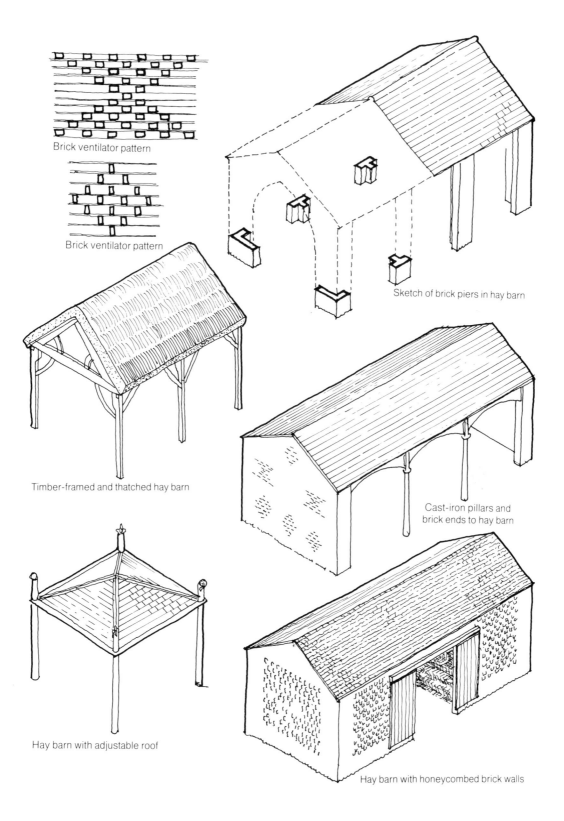

Brick ventilator pattern

Brick ventilator pattern

Sketch of brick piers in hay barn

Timber-framed and thatched hay barn

Cast-iron pillars and
brick ends to hay barn

Hay barn with adjustable roof

Hay barn with honeycombed brick walls

Chapter 6
Farmsteads

Farmstead patterns

We have seen how the design of individual farm buildings related so closely to the functions to be performed in them and we may expect that the design of the complete farmstead was equally functional. Two aspects may be considered: the arrangement of the farmstead as a whole and the relationship of the farmhouse to the farm buildings.

While there are many exceptions, resulting from topography and the accidents of historical development, eight patterns of farmstead may be distinguished, and haphazard, apparently formless layouts constitute a ninth. In the first two patterns the farmhouse and all farm buildings are combined in a line, both components being housed under the same roof. There are two versions and they are considered in more detail later as *longhouses* and *laithe-houses*. In the *parallel* arrangement, the farmhouse and a set of farm buildings were arranged in parallel, or nearly so; the farm buildings range might consist of barn, cow-house and stable with the farmhouse range probably incorporating a cartshed and granary. The association of the granary with the house is longstanding and was continued in the small farms on which this parallel arrangement is usually found. The larger farms, of 50 to 150 acres or so (22.3 ha. to 67 ha.) adopted L-shaped or U-shaped layouts, the barn providing shelter to the farmyard and, on the larger farms, shelter sheds helping to make up the U-shape. On the largest farms, of 250 acres or more (110 ha) the farm buildings extended round a farmyard completely enclosed as a *courtyard* or they made *several foldyards*. The numerous farm buildings of the largest farms resulted sometimes from a process of accretion, more buildings being added as more land came under increasingly productive cultivation, and sometimes from a process of deliberate planning, something which is clearly seen in the farmsteads depending on a mixing house which served several foldyards. In the eighth arrangement some or all of the farm buildings were combined in one structure so that the farmstead consisted of little more than the farmhouse and a *combination farm building* across the farmyard. The ninth category covers farmsteads of unplanned, or *haphazard* layout or of patterns which have not yet been recognised.

Although the larger farms generally have the more farm buildings and the more elaborate farmstead layouts this is not always so. A farm in East Anglia of large acreage and a heavy bias towards cereal crops might keep few cattle, probably in a foldyard, and with many sheep folded in the fields and requiring no housing, its farmstead might consist only of a large farmhouse, a large threshing barn, a small box-like granary and nothing else. Similarly, a farm in mountainous country might have a large nominal acreage much of which

78. Farmstead layout diagrams.

102

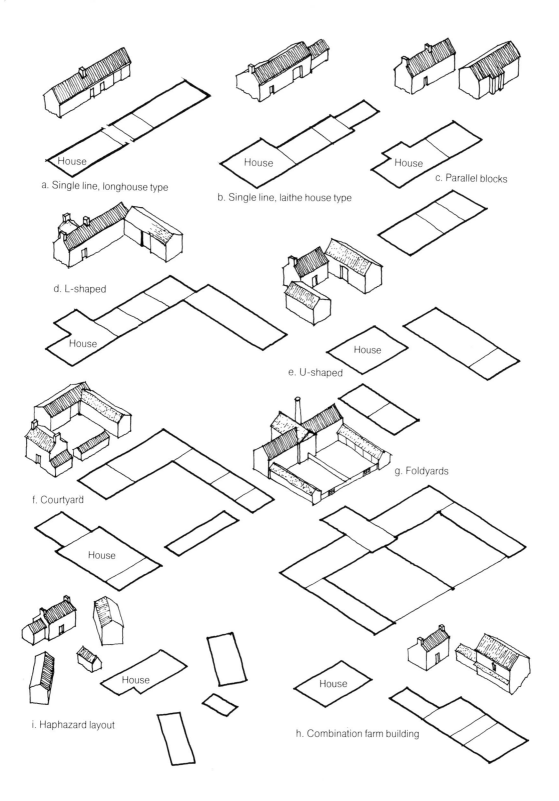

a. Single line, longhouse type

b. Single line, laithe house type

c. Parallel blocks

d. L-shaped

e. U-shaped

f. Courtyard

g. Foldyards

i. Haphazard layout

h. Combination farm building

House

consisted of rough grazing land supporting many sheep. For such a farm the L- or U-shaped farmstead generally found on a much smaller farm would be considered quite appropriate.

The relationship of farmhouse to farm buildings is worth some mention. In longhouse and laithe-house arrangements, the association is, of course, very close. In the parallel arrangement, also, some farm building may be attached to the farmhouse. In this and other layouts the farmhouse may be sandwiched between farm buildings. Otherwise the farmhouse is detached from farm buildings but may face on to the farmyard, back on to the farmyard, or be completely detached, the house, with its separate drive, disdaining the buildings and yard which justify its existence. In England and Wales attached farmhouse and farm buildings are most often found in the Pennines and the Lake Counties, and in Wales, and there are smaller concentrations in Cleveland and on Dartmoor. In these districts three-quarters or even more of the farmhouses have farm buildings attached. On the other hand it is very rare to find a farmhouse attached to farm buildings in the eastern and south-eastern counties; in Kent, for instance, whether the farmhouse is a fifteenth-century Wealden house or a nineteenth-century double-pile house it will stand quite apart from its farm buildings.

Where a farmhouse is detached, its association with farm buildings seems to be a matter of time and status; the more recent and more pretentious the house, the less likely is any association with the farmyard. Some agricultural writers recommended that the farmhouse, or at least the back door of the farmhouse, should face the farmyard so that the farmer could keep his eyes on his labourers and generally know what was happening in his farmyard. But apart from matters of supervision there was obviously some convenience in being able to relate the dairy and the kitchen to the cow-house and the pigsty.

Longhouses, laithe-houses and bastle houses

Accommodation for domestic and farming purposes has traditionally been placed under the same roof according to one of three fashions: longhouse, laithe-house and bastle house fashion. In the longhouse the farmhouse and cow-house are combined; in the laithe-house the farmhouse is integral with some sort of stable/barn/cow-house unit; in the bastle house the farmhouse lies above the cow-house.

The longhouse, in its varying degrees of purity, consists of a dwelling-house reached by way of a cross-passage which also provides the sole or a subsidiary means of access to a cow-house and its loft above. In one version, the cross-passage also acts as a feeding passage for cattle, between four and six in number, tethered nose on to the passage. In another version, the cow-house has its own front entrance but there is a door, or at least a hatch, whereby cattle may be reached or supervised. In a third version, the cows are tethered nose on to the side walls and tail on to a central manure passage which drains downhill through the end wall. The full significance of the cross-passage is still not completely understood. Both height and width vary in the surviving examples, but in no case are they sufficient for the passage to have served as a floor for hand flail threshing, though the more ancient devices of beating a single sheaf against a wall or partition and of treading out the grain with the hooves of cattle driven

79. House and farm building connections.

104

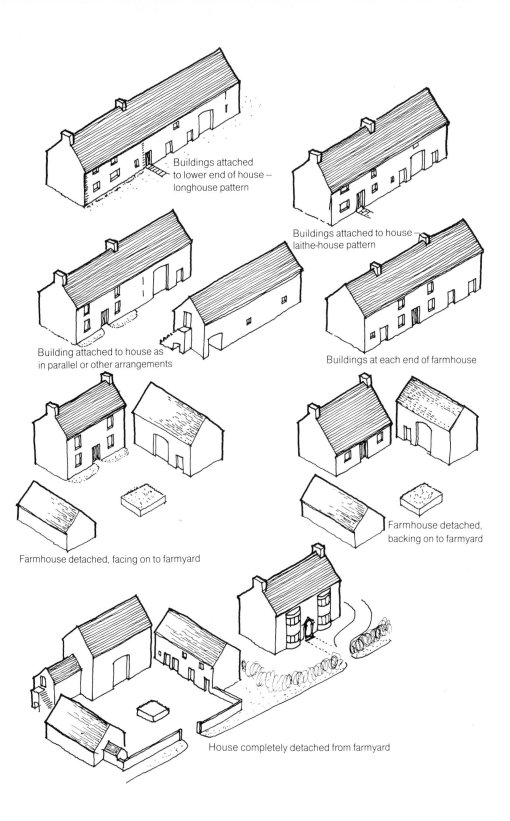

Buildings attached
to lower end of house –
longhouse pattern

Buildings attached to house –
laithe-house pattern

Building attached to house as
in parallel or other arrangements

Buildings at each end of farmhouse

Farmhouse detached, facing on to farmyard

Farmhouse detached,
backing on to farmyard

House completely detached from farmyard

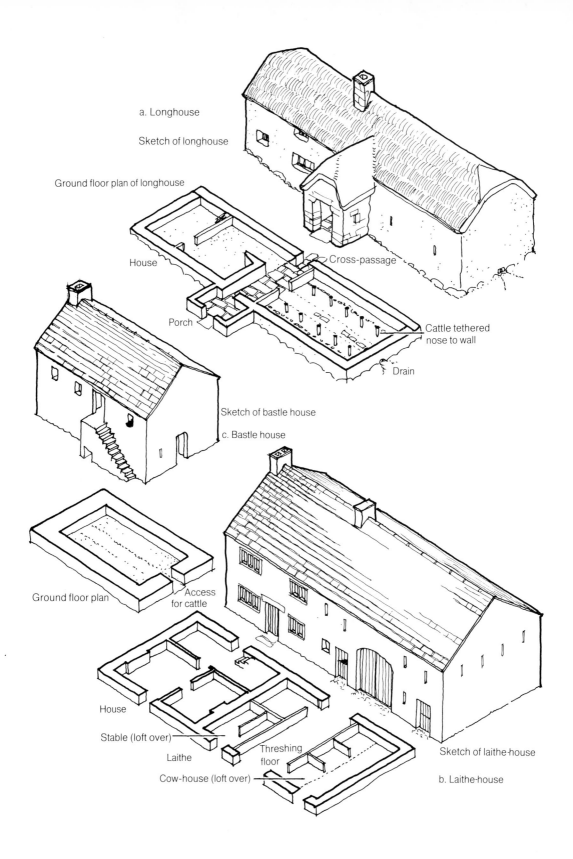

a. Longhouse

Sketch of longhouse

Ground floor plan of longhouse

House

Cross-passage

Porch

Cattle tethered
nose to wall

Drain

Sketch of bastle house

c. Bastle house

Ground floor plan

Access
for cattle

House

Stable (loft over)

Laithe

Threshing
floor

Cow-house (loft over)

Sketch of laithe-house

b. Laithe-house

to and fro could have been employed. It is not that the cross-passage was necessary for the access of both cattle and humans; other buildings which combine human and animal occupation – the 'black houses' of northern Scotland, for instance, manage without the cross-passage. In England and Wales, the cross-passage was, for some reason, considered structurally to be part of the cow-house for any break of roof or wall usually lies between cross-passage and house, though architecturally it was part of the house, sharing in any masonry details which might embellish the house.

The longhouse is a very ancient building type in this country. Excavations suggest that the standard medieval family farm may have consisted only of a longhouse and a small barn. Longhouses and their derivatives survive in Cumbria, Devon and north-east Yorkshire and a few other places in England and they survive in much of the southern half of Wales; somewhat similar combinations of house and cow-house were once widespread in Scotland, though without the cross-passage. Longhouses continued to be built in parts of England until well into the eighteenth century and, as we have seen, in Wales cow-houses were added to farmhouses with the aid of a cross-passage to give a longhouse-like building until quite late in the nineteenth century.

The laithe-house had had a shorter life and a more restricted distribution. The true laithe-house consists of a conventional domestic building of eighteenth or nineteenth century type (i.e. two rooms deep and one or two rooms wide) to which is attached a combination barn, table and cow-house of the same two-storey height. Thus the laithe-house, like the longhouse, is normally a simple elongated rectangle on plan. There is rarely any intercommunication between domestic and agricultural portions and the barn block is as likely to be attached to the parlour end of the house as to the kitchen end. The true laithe-house was built all at one time but, as with the longhouse, the form may be achieved by adding later farm buildings to an existing farmhouse.

80. Longhouses, laithe-houses and bastle houses

81. Longhouse at Lettaford, Devon Here the longhouse is built along a slope and the manure from the cow-house at the right drains away through the gable wall. The porch marks the entrance to the cross-passage.

82. Laithe-house near Todmorden, Yorkshire
The house and farm buildings form a single rectangular block under one roof but there is no cross-passage.

83. Bastle house, Tarset West, Northumberland
The access to the domestic part at the upper level is now by external staircase; access for the animals may be seen at the foot of the steps.

The laithe-house is found almost entirely on the Pennine slopes and mainly between the Aire Gap and the Peak District, though the type does stray northwards towards Northumberland and westwards into Bowland and Rossendale in Lancashire. There are examples from as early as 1650 and as late as 1880, but the great period of construction was between about 1780 and 1820. The building type seems to have grown out of a society which enjoyed the profitable combination of hand-powered textile work and part-time farming, which Daniel Defoe found so admirable on his tours in the early eighteenth century.

A bastle house differs from a longhouse or a laithe-house in that the division between domestic and agricultural uses is vertical rather than horizontal. In the bastle house a dwelling consisting of a larger and a smaller room with a partial or complete garret above was raised over a ground floor cow-house. Access to the dwelling-house was by a ladder or, later, by a fixed external staircase and through a heavily barred door in the front wall. Access to the cow-house was by a door, again heavily barred, usually in the gable wall but sometimes in the front. All surviving true bastle houses have stone walls of a defensive thickness of four feet (1.2 m) or so.

Bastle houses were indeed places of passive defence. They were occupied as farmhouses but in such a way that cattle barred in the lower floor and the family secure on the upper floor, behind a door which could not be battered down, need not fear rustlers or kidnappers. The building type flourished on the English side of the Scottish Border from the mid-sixteenth to the early seventeenth century, though some examples are older. Socially the occupier of a bastle house seems to have held a position between that of the local landowner, whose refuge was the castle or tower-house and whose cattle were secured within a defensible high-walled yard, and the general run of small farmers whose cattle and families would have to seek refuge elsewhere.

The bastle house type did not die out completely with the Union of the Crowns in 1603 or the political union of 1707. It seems that the tradition of living over cattle in warmth and security was not entirely lost to the Northumbrian people and a few instances have recently been recorded of houses placed over stables and cow-houses, though not, of course, for defensive purposes, during the eighteenth and nineteenth centuries.

Lancashire barns and some other combination barns

Changes in the role of the barn which accompanied the increasing productivity of the arable fields, as well as the increasing efficiency in converting sheaves of corn into grain and straw, led to a tendency to merge other building uses with the barn rather than having the barn as an isolated self-sufficient building on the farmstead. One combination of barn and cow-house is called here the Lancashire barn from the county in which it was first identified and where it is commonly found.

The Lancashire barn consists of a conventional hand flail threshing barn, usually of five bays, though sometimes of four bays, with a cow-house and loft replacing two storage bays to one side of the threshing floor. The cow-house is entered through the gable in which the tell-tale three doors reveal a central feeding passage and flanking manure passages. Sometimes the cow-house floor is slightly below the threshing floor level (giving a tall loft above) but usually it is on the same level.

It appears that the barn was used in the traditional way, sheaves taken from the full-height storage bays being threshed and winnowed on the floor between the opposed barn doors and straw being stacked on the loft until it could be dropped to the cow-house below. The cow-house was usually rather wider than the barn, the difference in roof span and eaves line being mastered with the aid of a projecting canopy sweeping down from the main roof and supported by cheeks at one side. The differences were so slight as to call attention to the traditions, stemming presumably from the different origins of the two types of building, amalgamated in the Lancashire barn.

Another combination barn widely used had lofts rather than full-height bays

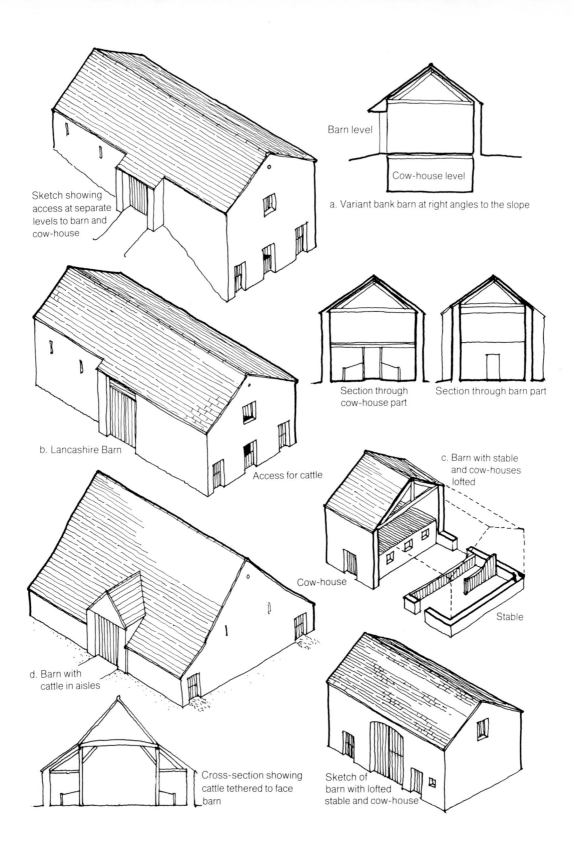

Sketch showing access at separate levels to barn and cow-house

a. Variant bank barn at right angles to the slope

Barn level

Cow-house level

b. Lancashire Barn

Section through cow-house part

Section through barn part

Access for cattle

c. Barn with stable and cow-houses lofted

Cow-house

Stable

d. Barn with cattle in aisles

Cross-section showing cattle tethered to face barn

Sketch of barn with lofted stable and cow-house

84. Some combination barns.

85. Connected farmhouse and farm buildings, Llanwddyn, Montgomeryshire The farmhouse is at one end of a range including a cow-house and granary/cartshed.

86. Lancashire Barn, near Lancaster, Lancashire The characteristic three doors in the gable leading to the cow-house may be seen and also the reduced width of the barn beyond the barn doors.

on each side of the threshing floor. One loft was over a stable and the other was over the cow-house. This combination suited the smaller farm, such as that occupied by a part-time farmer, for a limited amount of corn could be temporarily stored on one loft, threshed, and then consumed from the other loft practically as fast as it was threshed.

Both these combination barn types seem to date from the period between about 1750 and 1850 and although mainly associated with the north-west of England may be found in other parts of the country.

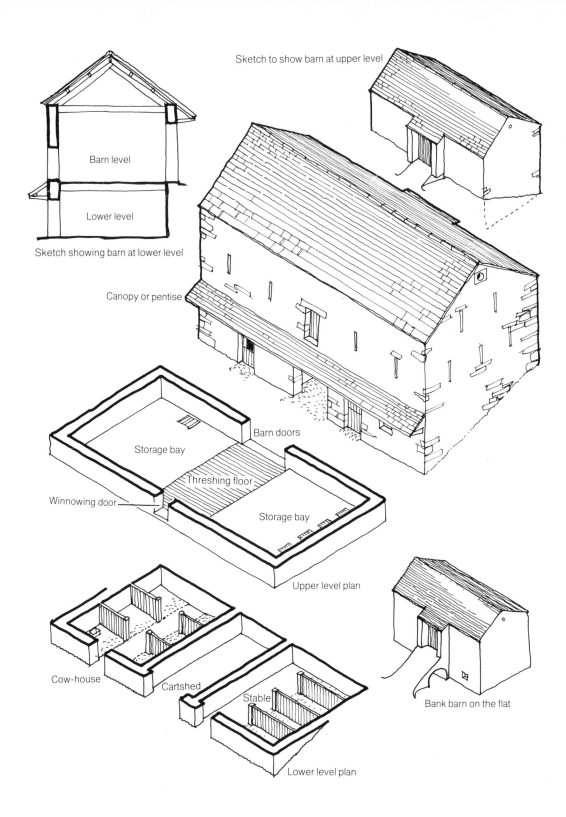

Sketch to show barn at upper level

Barn level

Lower level

Sketch showing barn at lower level

Canopy or pentise

Barn doors

Storage bay

Threshing floor

Winnowing door

Storage bay

Upper level plan

Cow-house

Cartshed

Stable

Lower level plan

Bank barn on the flat

112

Bank barns

Among the types of combination farm buildings, the bank barn is surely pre-eminent for its compactness, its economy, and, very often, its rugged beauty. The term 'bank barn' is, perhaps, unfamiliar. It is an American term used to describe that type of farm building which is a simple rectangular gabled structure on two levels, the upper level being a conventional threshing barn and the lower level comprising a series of spaces as, for instance, cow-house, stable, cartshed and loose box. The whole is sited along a natural or artificial slope in such a way that access may be gained from the fields or a road to the upper level and from the farmyard to the lower level. The American term has been imported into Britain to describe a type of combination farm building which is so common in certain parts of Britain that it has developed no descriptive term of its own.

The simple rectangular shape of the bank barn is, in fact, sometimes extended on its upper side wall through use of a projecting porch or canopy on cheeks around the barn doors or through the addition of small spaces, such as a cornhole or temporary granary covered by an extension of the main roof. The threshing barn at the upper level has the usual storage bays on each side of the threshing floor. All the floors are boarded, including the threshing floor, but the levels may vary according to what is beneath: a stable below may give a raised

87. Bank barns.

88. Bank barn near Crook, Westmorland This view from the lower or farmyard level shows the canopy or pentise protecting cow-house and stable doors and also shows the winnowing door high above.

89. Bank barn near Shap, Westmorland This view is of the upper or barn level; as the slope here is not very great there is a ramp to the doors and also extra access to the lower level.

floor above, for instance. The main barn doors open outwards at the head of a short ramp rising from a field or farm track: opposite there is a winnowing door opening inwards and situated precariously high above the farmyard level. The upper part is quite conventional in its use of ventilation slits, owl holes and so on, and seems to have been used quite conventionally as a hand flail threshing barn. On the lower level a common arrangement puts an open-fronted single-bay cartshed below the threshing floor, keeping this important part of the barn well ventilated and free from the stench of animals. Stables, cow-houses and loose boxes occupy the remainder of the lower level, but with their open doors protected in many cases by a continuous canopy or pentise carried on timber or stone beams which are cantilevered from the main wall.

Usually a bank barn is found along a slope, and the building type being characteristic of certain hilly districts slopes are not hard to find. Sometimes the bank barn is built on flat land when a long steep ramp extends high up to reach the barn doors. A variant on the bank barn lies at right angles to the slope, having only part of the lower level accessible. This variant seems to be related to the Lancashire barn and is, in fact, commonly found in the Lune valley.

As with so many farm building types, the bank barn was mainly a development of the eighteenth and nineteenth centuries, though recent research has suggested that prototypes were built in the seventeenth century on large farms. Dated examples are quite plentiful, ranging from the 1730s to the first few years of the twentieth century. It is hard to accept that the later examples were built for hand flail threshing even on remote upland sites difficult of access for the steam-powered threshing train. They do retain the winnowing door, and it is possible that from the 1870s onwards these barns were expected to accommodate hay, at least until the expected and long-awaited return to the mixed farming of earlier years took place.

The bank barn was economical in first construction since one roof and one set of foundations was saved over the two or more buildings otherwise required. It was also economical in labour insofar as the unprocessed crops were hauled easily into the upper level and straw, or later hay, could be dropped through hatches into the cow-house and stable. A family farm need consist of only two buildings: a farmhouse with provision for a little grain storage, and a bank barn with a yard and midden between.

The bank barn was thus a suitable combination farm building for use in hilly districts where farms were small, arable areas always limited, where the whole cereal crop was embarned at one time, and where suitable slopes were always available. In fact, the main concentration lies in Cumbria, especially in the Lake District, Pennine Cumbria and the West Cumberland Plain. In these districts bank barns abound so that practically every farm has one and few conventional or flat barns are to be seen. There are even some bank barns on artificial slopes in parts of north-west Cumberland. Distribution of the building type spreads out just over the Pennines, though not into the Yorkshire Dales generally. Southwards the occasional bank barn may be seen in hilly North Lancashire but not usually much below the Lune Valley. Another much smaller and less dense concentration occurs in Devon, but otherwise, apart from some few examples in Scotland, this admirably economical building type is not found in Britain. Careful search in the Peak District and throughout Wales has brought forward no true examples even though these regions have a similar topography and had similar farming to Cumbria.

The term 'bank barn' was introduced from North America because the building type was developed to a high degree of perfection in Pennsylvania, in parts of adjacent states and in territories settled from Pennsylvania. In fact multi-level barns are wide-spread throughout northern and north-eastern USA. The severe winter climate meant that all stock had to be housed, that all crops preferably were housed, including root crops, and that even the manure was best kept within a building. The typical New England barn, for instance, consists of a large threshing and hay barn, sometimes with lofts on two levels, raised over a large cow-house and stable, which were raised in turn over a semi-basement, part root cellar and part manure cellar. These barns, however, were usually entered from the gable and were related in various ways to flat or sloping land.

The perfected American bank barn, often called the Pennsylvania barn, had the same characteristics as those listed for its British counterpart, but it was usually much bigger, and, in addition, it usually had a 'forebay', a cantilevered section of the upper level which served to protect the doors of the floor below (like the English canopy or pentise) but which also served to increase the capacity of the barn above. Not all Pennsylvania bank barns have a forebay nor are all forebays cantilevered – some are carried on columns – but certainly the forebay is generally characteristic of the Pennsylvania barn. Most of the barns now to be seen are timber-framed, usually over a stone ground floor; some are of brick, some are entirely of stone except for a timber-framed forebay; early examples, recorded in photographs and contemporary descriptions, were made of horizontal log construction. Many are brightly coloured, especially those in the Pennsylvania Dutch country, around Lancaster and York. Dated examples range from 1754 onwards but most are nineteenth century, extending right through the century, still being advocated in books of barn plans right into the early twentieth century and still being built right up to the present day by members of some of the strict Protestant sects, such as the Amish.

It has generally been assumed that the Pennsylvania barn was introduced to North America by settlers attracted by William Penn to the State from Germany and particularly from the Rhineland-Palatinate region. Recent fieldwork by two American scholars working independently suggests that east central Switzerland is a more likely source since barns with the forebay feature, though not necessarily on banks, may be seen there. The surviving examples do not seem to be ancient but the forebay tradition was evidently present. It is tempting to press an English origin for the Pennsylvania barn since dated English bank barns are earlier than reliably dated American examples, and since there were strong family connections and strong trade links between Cumbria and North America throughout the late seventeenth and eighteenth centuries, including links between Penn himself and the Fells of Swarthmoor right in the heart of bank barn country. But as long as the forebay is considered an essential characteristic of the Pennsylvania bank barn the connection cannot be pressed.

The bank barn is found in a few other parts of Europe, in Norway and central France, for instance, but not in countries with any strong recent historical links with either Britain or the relevant parts of North America.

Field barns and outfarms

On some farms both in hilly and lowland districts the total complement of farm buildings is not concentrated in the farmstead, some being dispersed as outfarms or field barns. An outfarm has some accommodation for crops and animals together with a foldyard and so makes a small building group; a field barn consists of a single building housing crops and animals but without a foldyard.

As long as farms consisted of cultivated crops in open fields together with meadows and grazing rights on surrounding pastures there was every advantage in siting the farmstead in the centre of the community in the village or hamlet. Once most or all of the land was enclosed and cultivated the situation was quite different. The farmstead might now be at one end of the allocated land; an enclosure award might have given a substantial portion of land to the

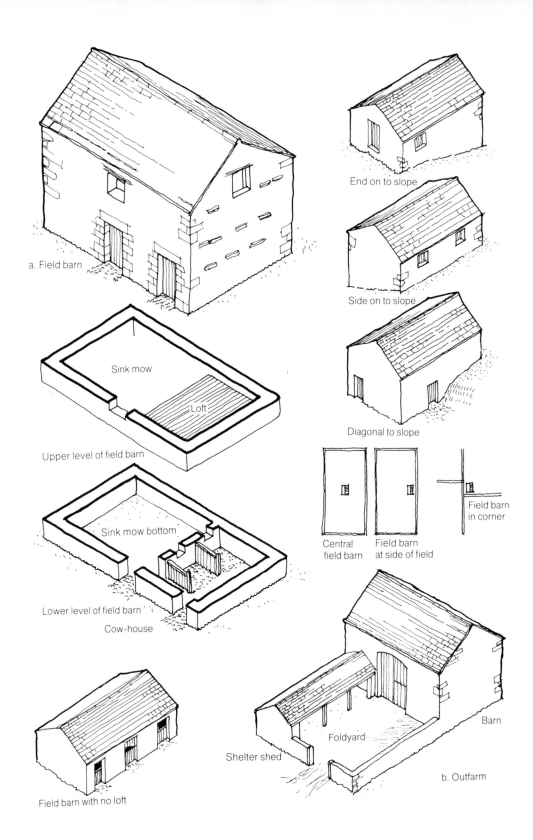

a. Field barn

End on to slope

Side on to slope

Diagonal to slope

Sink mow

Loft

Upper level of field barn

Sink mow bottom

Lower level of field barn

Cow-house

Central field barn

Field barn at side of field

Field barn in corner

Field barn with no loft

Shelter shed

Foldyard

Barn

b. Outfarm

90. **Field barns and outfarms.**

91. **General view of field barns near Thwaite, Yorkshire** The farmsteads nestle in the valley bottom while the field barns are set in the valley slopes and served the newly enclosed fields.

farm distant from the ancient lands belonging to it; the farmstead might be of new foundation with much of its enclosed land on the upland slopes; the farm might have grown through amalgamation with others unable to adapt to new farming conditions, and so many parts might be distant from a central farmstead. In circumstances such as these, satellites such as field barns or outfarms might make the working of the farm easier and more economical.

The main saving was in travel and transport. Normally, crops would have to be carried from all parts of the farm to the farmstead and manure returned to all the cultivated fields, however distant. Where the outlying land was high on the hill slopes and the farmstead down in the valley, crops were shaken and lost on the journey down and heavy manure made the return journey hard and irksome. There was obviously an advantage if crops could be consumed where they were grown and manure deposited where it was produced.

In the field barn the usual arrangement was to feed hay to young cattle. The hay was cut from the enclosed fields as part of the rotation; it was carted or simply swept into a loft or sink mow at an upper level; throughout the winter it

92. Field barn near Muker, Yorkshire This building is set on the flat but has a hay loft above a loose box for cattle. Projecting 'through stones' may be seen in the wall.

was dropped from the loft or drawn from the sink mow to feed to heifers or bullocks shut in a loose box or to cows tied in a cow-house. The manure built up in the loose box or cleared from the cow-house was then spread on the adjacent fields and cultivation as part of crop rotation could begin again with the spring.

The relationship between crop storage and animal housing varied quite considerably. Sometimes, as in Derbyshire, Leicestershire, Staffordshire and in Wensleydale in Yorkshire, there was no loft and the hay was presumably kept in a haystack until the existing rough small Dutch barns were built. In other examples the whole of the ground floor was devoted to cattle while there was a tall capacious hay loft filled from pitching holes. A design popular in the Yorkshire Dales had half the lower floor as a loose box and the other half as a sink mow, merging with the loft at its upper level. Sometimes, two sink mows flanked a cow-house. Generally the designs depended on the storage and consumption of hay but tall barn doors and what are patently threshing floors in some field barns suggest that hand flail threshing and the production of straw was important.

The field barn required daily attention. Someone had to feed and water and exercise the cattle and someone had to milk cows when necessary, taking the milk back to the farmyard in a back-packed churn. If there was corn in the field barn then some had to be threshed every day. Field barns certainly did not eliminate labour but they substituted a little light hill walking for difficult journeys with carts over steep tracks.

Field barns are generally found alongside a wall or fence about halfway up a sloping field. In such a location the barn would serve two adjacent fields, half the crops could be swept down the slope from the upper half of the field and half the manure could be spread down the lower half of the field, carting would be confined to taking up half the hay crop to the field barn and half the manure heap to the upper fields. Sometimes field barns are to be found in the bottom corner of a field, serving it and three adjacent fields. Sometimes the field barn may be found in the centre of a single large field. Although some field barns were built on the flat most were set on a slope, either end on or side on to the slope; the former arrangement is best for the smaller barn with a gable access to the loft; the latter arrangement is best for a larger barn with pitching holes.

Although few examples bear dates, field barns generally seem to belong to the period from the mid-eighteenth century to just before the middle of the nineteenth

93. Outfarm near Fittleworth, Sussex This little building has space for cattle and opened onto a foldyard.

94. Outfarm at Romden, Kent The group includes a barn (now altered) and a shelter shed serving a foldyard.

119

century and seem to be closely related to statutory enclosure of common land. They are most characteristic of the Yorkshire Dales, and especially Swaledale, whose slopes are spattered with field barns as if a giant had spilled his box of Lego houses. They are found in other upland areas, in Derbyshire for instance, and in Devon, as well as in Snowdonia.

A common arrangement for the outfarm was a barn storing hay or corn, a foldyard with a shelter shed, a stable, perhaps, and sometimes a labourer's cottage. In such an arrangement a labourer could spend the winter months tending the loose cattle in the foldyard, threshing a daily ration of grain and straw, and exercising the horses on whatever work was required in that season. Outfarms were often recommended by nineteenth-century writers because of their savings on transport, and they may be seen in most of the midland counties of England.

Neither outfarms nor field barns have much part to play in present day farming. The tractor and the Land Rover have much reduced transport problems, home-threshed corn is less important as fodder, silage has much diminished the importance of hay, artificial fertilisers have reduced the importance of manure and few labourers or their families would be happy to live the lonely life of the isolated and poorly serviced outfarm. Yet outfarms to some extent, and field barns to a very considerable extent, play a major part in the make-up of the rural landscape.

95. Outfarm buildings, Cwm du, Breconshire
These buildings are set on a slope well away from the main farmstead.

Minor farmyard structures

As well as the major buildings ranged round the farmyard there were other buildings and structures of various sorts which played some minor, but often quite interesting, part in the organisation of the farmyard. Among these may be mentioned the dairy, the slaughterhouse, the ash-house, the bee-boles and the causeway.

The *dairy* was not always a distinct farmyard building. Often, probably mostly, it was a part of the farmhouse, facing north, well-ventilated and equipped with cold stone slabs, and located near to the back door which led to the farmyard. Sometimes, however, the dairy was a separate building and more part of the farm buildings than the domestic. On model farms and the home farms of large estates the dairy was a substantial and a well-decorated building, often octagonal on plan. On most working farms, however, it was much more plain and utilitarian in design.

On the ordinary farm the dairy had the same provision as that of the purely domestic dairy but needed plenty of space for the temporary storage of milk, for separating the cream from the milk, and for the weekly churning into butter. In the more purely dairying regions where the production of farmhouse cheese was important the dairy also served as the cheese-making plant, with space for the tuns or kettles in which the milk was heated before curdling, space for the wooden cheese-vats, and space for the heavy cheese press. The products of the cheese-making dairy were kept in racks in a well-ventilated cheese room, and turned daily until ready for the market.

The *slaughterhouse* was not often found on the smaller farmsteads but was sometimes provided on the larger or remote farmsteads. A slaughterhouse was useful where many animals were kept, where some might have to be killed following accidents and where a communal slaughterhouse was not available.

96. Slaughterhouse, Cowfold, Sussex The slaughterhouse building has brick walls and a Horsham slate roof.

97. Skep or bee-hive hole, Manaton, Devon Recesses for bee-hives may often be found in farmyard walls.

But provision of a slaughterhouse assumed that someone on the farm was skilled at the trade and that the meat could be consumed in the household or could be easily traded. No special provision seems to have been required of the slaughterhouse except for height whereby the carcase might be hung and a nearby loose box or yard in which the animal could be kept before slaughter.

The *ash-house* was usually an isolated domical structure with a small doorway, found in the farmyard but near the farmhouse. Presumably the buildings were intended for the storage of domestic ash taken from the hearth and before it was scattered on the fields. The method of construction was possibly employed as a means of fire-proofing; the absence of timber in the walls and roof minimised the danger from hot ashes. Usually the general appearance and constructional system of the ash-house was similar to that of the domical corbelled pigsty, but in Devon such buildings were sometimes made with a turf roof which was flat rather than domed.

A *bee-bole* or bee-hole was a recess in the wall of a farmyard intended to contain the old hive or 'skep' in which bees were formerly housed. Sometimes the bee-bole had an arched head, rather like a crude Gothic niche, for straw skeps of the old-fashioned hives were pointed, but often the recess was simply square-headed. Usually there was a row of bee-boles; sometimes they were guarded by lockable iron grilles for the honey was valuable and, given co-operative bees, easily portable.

The *causeway*, as the name suggests, was a paved walk which connected the doors of the various buildings surrounding the farmyard. It was necessary in order to keep the manure deposited and trodden in the yard within some bounds, and on old farmsteads it tended to become a raised causeway as season after season the yard was cleared of manure and year after year a few inches of yard bottom went out with the last loads of manure.

98. Ash-house, Thorn, Devon This curious building on a circular plan is a type of ash-house often found in south-western England.

Chapter 7

Materials and construction

Introduction
Britain is blessed with a considerable variety of building materials and all have been used in farm buildings. Fields and quarries provided stone of all sorts, and the land yielded clay and timber and could be made to provide the raw materials for brick, tiles and thatch. Building materials being heavy and expensive to move it was the practice, until quite recently, to use the materials which were to hand for all the humble buildings of the farmstead. Often there was more than one material to hand – with timber growing above stone, straw for thatch being reaped from land bearing clay suitable for tiles, the choice of material seems to have been made as much for tradition and fashion as for economy.

The structural methods used for the construction of farm buildings have been and continue to be based on frame and mass. In frame construction the floor and roof loads were directed through the posts or other vertical elements of the frame safely to the ground; the wall was an enclosing element keeping out the rain and winds. Except that the frame may also constitute part of the wall the enclosing envelope could be omitted and the frame would still be stable. In mass construction the loads of roof and any intermediate floor were conducted through the walls to a foundation which also carried the weight of the floor itself. Without the wall the roof and floor could not be carried.

In the past, frame construction was virtually confined to timber-frame construction. In the box-frame and post-and-truss versions of timber-frame construction the structural members also formed part of the wall; in cruck construction the members were often hidden and the wall could be of any material. Mass wall construction has traditionally been of stone, of flint, cobble or pebbles, of brick or of clay. Generally one can assume that timber-frame construction was at some time used for farm buildings in all parts of Britain and its use has continued in some parts practically to the present day. Stone succeeded timber-frame in certain parts of the country, remaining in use for farm buildings until the later nineteenth century. Brick, while occasionally used with timber-frame, was generally introduced in farm building construction during the late seventeenth and early eighteenth centuries, while clay and earth of various sorts, including turf in Scotland, are of ancient use but continued to provide materials for farm buildings until well into the nineteenth century.

Cruck construction
Cruck construction is the term used for that method of timber building in which pairs of stout inclined timber members tied to make A-shaped frames were spaced at intervals along the barn or other farm building to collect roof loads by means of ridge, side purlins and wall plates and transmit them to the ground by

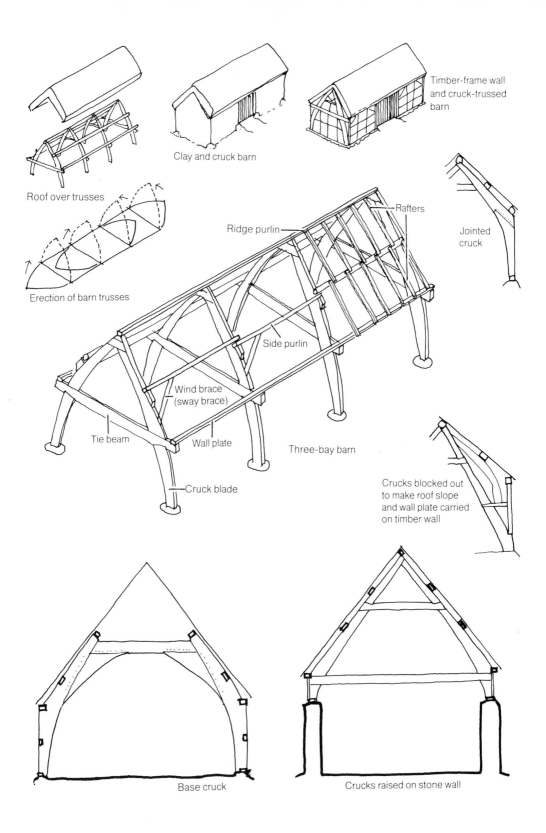

Roof over trusses

Clay and cruck barn

Timber-frame wall and cruck-trussed barn

Erection of barn trusses

Rafters

Ridge purlin

Jointed cruck

Side purlin

Wind brace (sway brace)

Tie beam

Wall plate

Three-bay barn

Cruck blade

Crucks blocked out to make roof slope and wall plate carried on timber wall

Base cruck

Crucks raised on stone wall

99. Cruck construction.

100. Cruck barn, Rainhill, Lancashire The cruck trusses are clearly to be seen here. The walls were probably of timber-frame originally, but this has been partly replaced by stone.

way of sill or padstones. In basic cruck construction the horizontal tie beam projected beyond the inclined cruck blades in order to carry the wall plates, while the ridge was carried in one of various ways at the apex of the cruck blades and the side purlins were supported directly or indirectly on the edges of the blades.

Often sawn from a single tree trunk to make a matching pair, the blades might be straight or distinctly elbowed but usually they were slightly curved and had a natural taper from base to apex. Although ridge and purlins gave longitudinal restraint, extra members were often introduced between purlins and cruck blades as 'wind braces' or 'sway braces'. Such cruck frames have been used for farm buildings in all of England and Wales and much of Scotland (apart from a closely defined portion of the eastern and south-eastern counties of England) from the early medieval period until the seventeenth century. Some derivatives were used in granaries, for example, until fairly late in the eighteenth century.

One variation, found only in a few early barns on important farms, is the base cruck. This consists of cruck blades which do not reach the apex of the roof but end at a stout collar above which there is a separate roof construction. Another variation, found especially in parts of West Wales and in the south-western counties of England and in Western Scotland, is the jointed cruck in which the blades are in two parts pegged together. A further variation leaves the cruck trusses at each end of the building truncated at collar level to allow a thatched roof to be swept in a half hip. Upper crucks terminated the blades in a horizontal beam carried by a stone or other mass wall; the upper cruck truss was rather like a simple roof truss but with curved feet to the principal rafters; it was a popular truss for granary roof spaces.

The walls, which in cruck construction carried no loads, could be of timber frame with panels of wattle or wattle and daub but were often of stone, brick or clay. In each case the walls were constructed traditionally and need give no sign of the crucks inside. Eventually it was realised that the wall could carry some of

125

the roof loads, and wall plates were carried by a wall rather than a frame, but were still tied to the cruck trusses by means of a spur or tie.

Cruck trusses were assembled on site and then 'reared' vertically into position, an occasion which called for the labour of friends and neighbours and so provided an excuse for a celebration. Cruck-trussed buildings were quick and easy to erect, had very simple joints and so made few demands on the carpenter's skill. They were inflexible, however, could not easily be used in two-storey construction and were difficult to extend sideways. Some trusses were of very considerable span, especially in barns – Leigh Court Barn in Worcestershire is thirty-four feet (10 m) wide – but such spans required enormous trees which became increasingly difficult to find. Among farm buildings cruck construction is most often found in barns, as an adequate span and height could be readily obtained, while the array of the beams and collars did not interfere with the functions of the barn. The construction is less often found in other farm buildings though, as already mentioned, upper crucks are found in granaries where the curved timbers gave a good run of uninterrupted headroom.

Box-frame and post-and-truss construction

Whereas in cruck construction the main purpose of the timber members is to carry the roof loads, in box-frame construction the members are framed together to make up a wall and it is the wall that carries roof loads; in post-and-truss construction the framing is similar but each bay of the wall construction is carried up as a roof truss and so the roof loads are, as in cruck construction, concentrated at bay intervals.

In both box-frame and post-and-truss construction studs and rails were added to posts to form the frame of a wall whose panels were infilled or were covered with some cladding material. The studs in nineteenth-century farm buildings may be of uniform cross-section, as indeed they are in modern timber-framed farm buildings, but in earlier centuries it was more common to divide the walled box into stout posts and lighter studs and rails. Opposite walls were held together by means of heavy timber beams which spanned from post to post. The timber box of several bays was stabilised with the aid of wall plates which ran horizontally at the head of each wall, locked into position by the tie beams, bay by bay. Straight or slightly curved bracing members helped to give longitudinal stability to the timber-framed wall.

Since the four walls of the building formed a rigid box the roof was a separate piece of construction, the roof covering being carried on pairs of rafters or a combination of rafters and roof truss. In the trussed rafter roof each pair of rafters was separately triangulated with the aid of a collar. This technique was adequate for carrying the roof loads but less satisfactory in terms of general stability for, in the absence of members to give longitudinal restraint, the roof was liable to collapse lengthways. The collar purlin gave just this longitudinal restraint. A collar purlin is a heavy timber plate running horizontally underneath the line of collars and supported at bay intervals by a short post called a crown post, which rises from the tie beam. Usually there were pairs of braces running longitudinally between the crown post and the collar purlin and laterally between the crown post and the collar immediately above. Sometimes the crown post was further supported by other braces rising from the tie beam to

101. Box-frame construction.

126

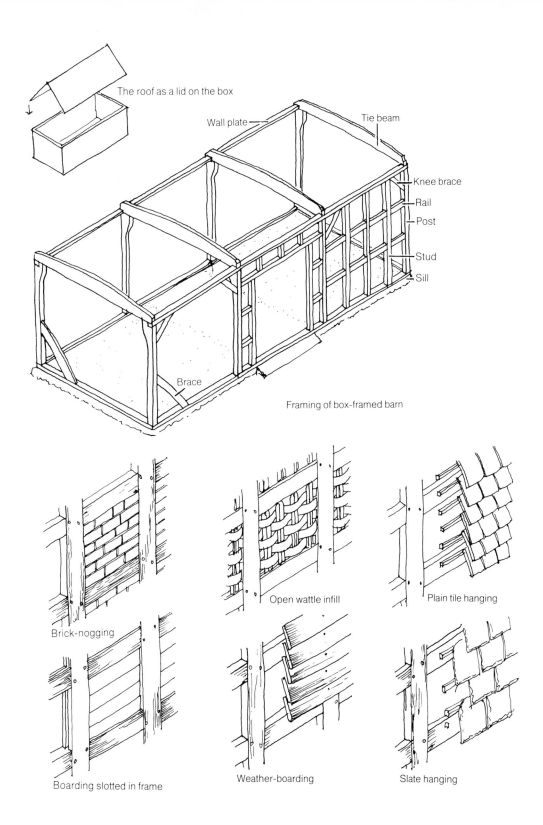

The roof as a lid on the box

Wall plate

Tie beam

Knee brace

Rail

Post

Stud

Sill

Brace

Framing of box-framed barn

Brick-nogging

Open wattle infill

Plain tile hanging

Boarding slotted in frame

Weather-boarding

Slate hanging

meet the crown post. This form of construction was often used in aisled barns, the common rafters extending out to meet the aisle walls.

In post-and-truss construction heavy pairs of principal rafters rose from each tie beam near its junction with the wall posts; the principal rafters and the tie beam made up the roof truss. Between each pair of trusses, purlins provided longitudinal restraint and also gave some support to common rafters. These purlins were either jointed into the principal rafters or were trapped between a principal rafter and a collar. Because the principal rafters, tie beam and posts ran together at intervals along the timber-framed walls of the barn, or other building, the structure may be considered a frame of posts and trusses all interlocked with the aid of the wall plates.

The post-and-truss technique was particularly suitable for barn construction. The tall walls with their stout posts at bay intervals gave great storage capacity to the barns and if the upper roof construction was rather complex this did not matter since the less accessible roof spaces might only be needed for storage in exceptional years. The box-frame and post-and-truss techniques were quite suitable for multi-storey buildings and so may be found in lofted stables and cow-houses and in granaries. In a few quite late instances both cruck and post-and-truss techniques were used in the same building: cruck trusses for a barn and post-and-truss for a cow-house, stable or granary under the same roof.

Infill and cladding to timber-frame construction

Whatever the structural technique the frame was not left open as a rule but was infilled or clad. Infilling consisted of material occupying each panel but not concealing the framing of the panel. The most common infill in domestic buildings was wattle and daub, and this was used in farm buildings also, but where ventilation was needed the daub was omitted and the panel was filled

102. **Box-frame walling, Hodnet, Shropshire** This large, well-preserved building is of timber-frame construction and has walls of square panels. Many panels retain their timber boards set in grooves between the studs and rails; other panels have been filled with brick-nogging.

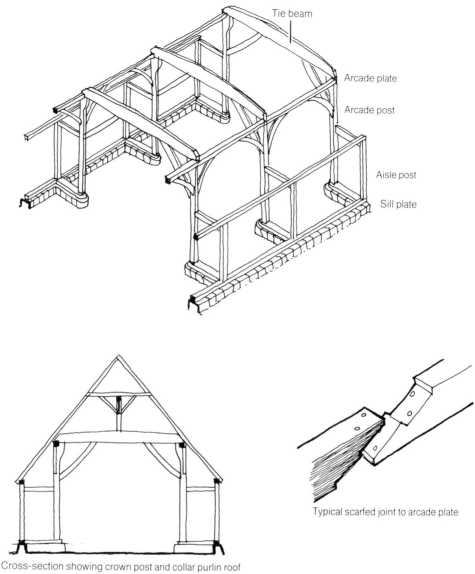

Tie beam

Arcade plate

Arcade post

Aisle post

Sill plate

Cross-section showing crown post and collar purlin roof

Typical scarfed joint to arcade plate

103. Aisled barn construction.

with a weave of wattlework. Examples of this technique are common in Shropshire and Herefordshire. Alternatively, the panels were filled with timber boards, not the weather-board of cladding but boards which were let into grooves in the studs and butted one board on top of another. Late infilling was brick nogging, often with an additional pattern of ventilation holes in the brickwork, and this material also replaced timber or wattle filling. Cladding was used when the timber members were to be entirely concealed by a weather-protective skin. This usually consisted of plain roofing tiles or slates or horizontal boarding: the plaster cladding found on timber-framed houses was not often used on farm buildings. Weather-boarding as now seen on farm buildings is usually fairly recent, but the technique and the use of black stain or tar does seem to have been in use for a couple of centuries or so.

Mud and stud construction

The vast majority of timber-framed farm buildings conform to the cruck or box-frame and post-and-truss techniques, but there is a further method of using timber which may be seen on humble buildings of late date and may be a testimony to a very old-established form of construction. This mud and stud technique consists of an open framework of rough posts rising from padstones at bay intervals or of earth-fast posts connected together with rough wall plates and tie beams. Spans were short and simple rafter roofs were quite adequate. The walls of storey height and bay width were not divided into panels but consisted of clay daubing about four inches (100 mm) thick reinforced with staves. Such mud and stud buildings are known in Lincolnshire, Leicestershire and lowland parts of Lancashire but may be found to be more extensively distributed. The construction was suitable for cheap and short-lived buildings, as it required little use of the carpenter's skill, and it may have been employed for centuries before our present substantial farm buildings were erected. Even in the eighteenth and nineteenth centuries the technique seems to have remained in use, but was used generally for loose boxes and shelter sheds or more substantial farm buildings – or those of more than one storey.

Roof construction for solid-walled farm buildings

So far, roof construction has been considered only in terms of timber-framed buildings, but many of the same constructional devices were used in roofing solid-walled structures. Trussed rafters, for instance, whether used alone or steadied by crown post and collar purlin, were used on solid walls and the tie beam was just as useful in keeping together solid walls of stone, brick or clay as tying the posts of timber-framed walls. Triangulated trusses of various sorts were carried on solid walls as the combination of principal rafters and tie beam served equally well in mass and framed construction.

Certain forms of roof construction, however, are more often seen with solid walls than as components in timber-frame construction: the king post roof truss, for instance, consisted of a heavy tie beam from which there rose a stout post carrying a ridge purlin and receiving the tops of principal rafters which in turn carried the side purlins. Inclined struts were usually fitted between the king post and the principal rafters, and sometimes the ridge was strutted back to the king posts. The king post roof truss was in continuous use from late medieval to modern times in superior farm buildings until it was superseded by steel roof trusses, though there were changes, especially in the method of joining the base of the king post to the centre of the tie beam during that period.

As stone and brick came more and more into use, some designers of farm buildings eliminated the roof truss entirely. The purlins were carried by pointed or semi-circular arches linked to the main wall of the building. Such arches performed double work in carrying the roof loads and at the same time buttressing the walls or piers. This construction was used in barns, especially

104. Roof construction.

130

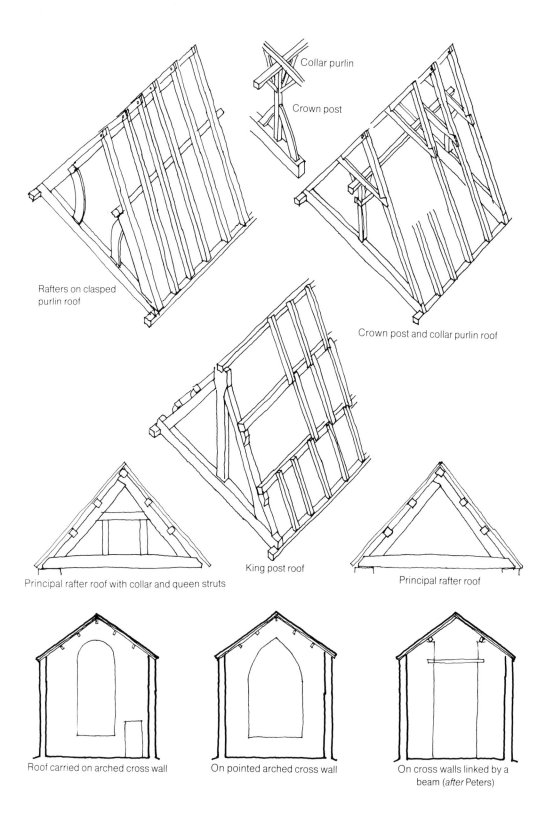

Collar purlin

Crown post

Rafters on clasped
purlin roof

Crown post and collar purlin roof

King post roof

Principal rafter roof with collar and queen struts

Principal rafter roof

Roof carried on arched cross wall

On pointed arched cross wall

On cross walls linked by a
beam (*after* Peters)

late barns with intermediate floors on each side of the central bay, and in hay barns, where the Gothic arches sit oddly among the trusses of hay.

Solid walls generally

We usually associate timber with timber-frame construction but in some parts of the world and at some times solid *timber* walls have been used for all forms of building construction: witness the log buildings of Scandinavian and Alpine countries, for instance. More and more evidence from excavated sites is beginning to suggest that vertical log walls were built in this country but no farm buildings with solid timber walls have survived. Solid walls here are confined to stone, brick and earth or clay. Until fairly recently, solid wall construction was confined to buildings of prestige or defensive nature, the rest were timber-framed or had some impermanent construction, but solid walls have been used throughout the period from which came the great majority of our stock of farm buildings.

Stone, flint, cobble and pebble

Stone has always been used for the most prestigious farm buildings, principally the monastic tithe barns, and good quality building stone was carried by water considerable distances to areas where stone was absent or poor. Where stone is easily quarried or found as outcrop it was used for farm buildings as well as houses, and over more than half of Britain most of the surviving farm buildings erected before the mid to late nineteenth century include some masonry construction.

Techniques used by the mason and waller in such humble buildings were simple and unsophisticated but the age of many of the buildings shows that they were effective. Usually the largest and best stones were raised at the corners of the building as alternating quoins, the inferior stones used in general walling having been laid to show the best surface on the face while tailing into the heart of the wall. Bonding stones or 'throughs' were laid at intervals to keep the inner and outer faces of the walls together, and in many farm buildings, especially in the Pennines and Cumbria, the through stones were not dressed back but project from the walls like a series of interrupted ledges. Stones were bedded in lime mortar, where available, or in clay where, as often as not, the better and more expensive mortar could not be used. Stones laid 'dry', that is without any mortar at all, were used for farm buildings in Cumbria and Snowdonia and some other mountainous districts. In areas which could yield sandstones or gritstones or substantial slatey stones the door and window openings were marked with dressed stone, but elsewhere simple wooden lintels and heavy wooden door jambs are to be seen. Where stone was too hard to dress or too soft to retain a dressing, then bricks were employed to substitute for dressings. Late nineteenth-century farm buildings in stone-bearing districts often show this use of bricks.

Sometimes the stone walls were whitewashed or rendered. This had some useful purpose in helping to prevent the leaching of soft mortar from the joints between stones but generally rendering or whitewashing seems to have been a matter of pride, distinguishing a well-kept farmstead from one of lesser quality.

Flint is found in some districts, especially of east and south-eastern England which lack good building stone. Flint proved a fairly satisfactory material for

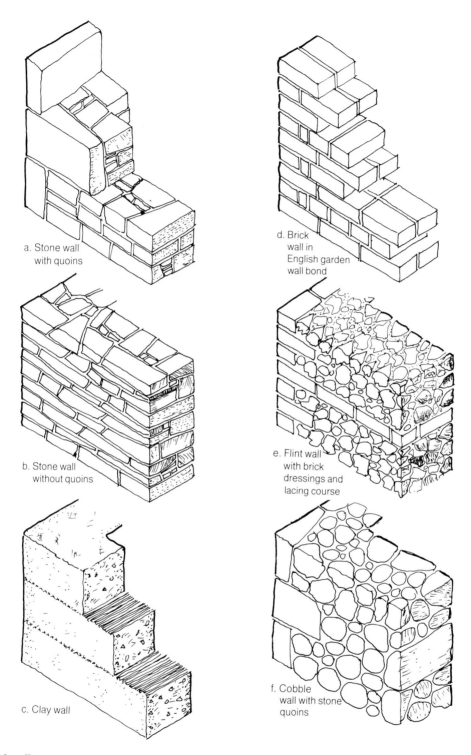

a. Stone wall
with quoins

b. Stone wall
without quoins

c. Clay wall

d. Brick
wall in
English garden
wall bond

e. Flint wall
with brick
dressings and
lacing course

f. Cobble
wall with stone
quoins

**105. Solid wall
construction.**

133

general walling but brick lacing courses were needed for stability and brick dressings were needed to form the corners and openings. Split or knapped flint cut so that the black interior faced outwards were used on the more pretentious farm buildings, in Norfolk for instance.

Cobbles and pebbles have similar defects and virtues to flint. Cobbles were used in the absence of good quarried stone and were found in river beds or as fieldstones in areas of morainic deposit. The rounded cobbles could only be used in walling with the aid of bonding stones which ran along the wall as well as across it, and with liberal use of clay mortar. Cobbles may be split like flint to give a flat face to the wall and this technique was used in the Lake District, for example, but the rounded tail within the wall thickness does little to ensure stability.

Whatever the type of stone used, there is no doubt that much of the attraction of farm buildings lies in the way in which structures of simple and straightforward planning are given life and variety through the colours and textures of their masonry walls.

Cob and other earthen walls

The cob walls of Devon and Cornwall are well known and many farm buildings in those counties were built in that material, but earthen walls under other names (such as mud, clay, wychert etc.) have been used in several other parts of Britain.

In cob or earth construction, the usual practice was to mix a suitable clay, dug from the site of the building, with dung and chopped straw until a stiff but pliable mass had been created. Batches of the material were placed around the line of the intended structure until a 'lift' of about two or three feet (610 or 914 mm) had been raised. This was pared to the required thickness and then allowed to dry and harden, layers of straw having been used to control the drying, and the chopped straw in the mixture having helped to control the shrinkage cracks. The process was repeated until the required height of wall had been achieved. It was a slow process, but if properly conducted a solid and stable wall was the result, and one which could have an indefinite life as long as a daub of plaster and whitewash kept the surface secure from rainwater.

Many farm buildings, especially barns and cow-houses, built in Devon, Cornwall, Leicestershire, Northamptonshire and Cumberland, as well as in parts of western Wales and the Lleyn Peninsula and in the south-west of Scotland, were made of clay. Usually the roofloads were carried by full or jointed crucks but the quality of clay walling was such that roof trusses could be carried on walls independently.

In East Anglia, clay was used in a different way. Many of the smaller farm buildings of early nineteenth century date were made of sun-dried clay block, laid like present day concrete blocks and then covered with a plaster rendering.

In Scotland, and especially in the northern and western parts, turf was pared from the fields and used to make walls either alone, in layers alternating between stones or as a thick core to stone linings.

Brick walling

While stone walling may be represented in the greatest area, brick walling probably covers the greatest number of farm buildings if only because the spread of brickwork in areas of timber-framing was so complete during the eighteenth and nineteenth centuries.

Good clay and earth for brickmaking is plentiful in most parts of England and is found in some parts of Wales and Scotland. Technical improvements during the nineteenth century widened further the types of raw material which could be made into bricks and made brick production relatively cheap. At the same time the railways enabled coal to be taken to the local brickworks and bricks to be taken from large brickworks to all but the most remote parts of Britain. Straightforward brickwork is also relatively simple to construct and, while no-one could deny the skill exercised by the bricklayers as craftsmen, the work required on farm buildings was generally of an unpretentious and undemanding nature. Brick-walled farm buildings were cheap and easily erected.

Brick sizes were never completely standardised; even now there are some regional and local variations in brick sizes, but early bricks were irregular and required thick mortar joints. Early brickwork also showed some variation in brick bonding, but gradually brickwork in farm buildings, as in other forms of construction, settled round variations of English and Flemish bonds. True English bond with alternate layers of headers and stretchers was not much used in farm buildings, but English Garden Wall bond with two or more courses of stretchers between the headers was much used and became the normal bond used by bricklayers in the northern counties of England. There were commonly either three or five courses of stretchers between the header courses. Flemish bond with its alternate headers and stretchers in each course was used in walls, especially where a good show was desired, but, again, variations of the bond whereby there were several stretchers between each pair of headers or several courses of stretchers between each course of alternate headers and stretchers was the technique most characteristic of farm buildings. Flemish bond and its variations was the bond normally used by bricklayers in the eastern, southern and midland counties of England.

Rat-trap bond (sometimes called Chinese bond) used bricks laid on edge rather than on the flat to produce a wall with internal cavities. Such a wall was not as strong as a solid wall but it used fewer bricks and so the technique was employed in simple farm buildings which were low and carried no great loads. The bond was also used in farmyard walls. There are concentrations of examples of this bond in Hampshire and in East Anglia but examples, usually of the early or mid-nineteenth century, may be seen practically anywhere in the southern half of England.

The most spectacular brickwork in farm building construction is shown in the walls of late barns, hay barns and hay lofts where the bricklayers delighted in making intricate patterns of ventilation holes.

Roofing materials

Of all the materials which could be used to cover the roofs of farm buildings, thatch was at one time the most commonly used. Where available, stone tiles, stone flags or natural slates were used for superior buildings such as the larger barns or stables. Plain tiles have a long history in the south-eastern counties of England and their use spread to the midland counties during the eighteenth and

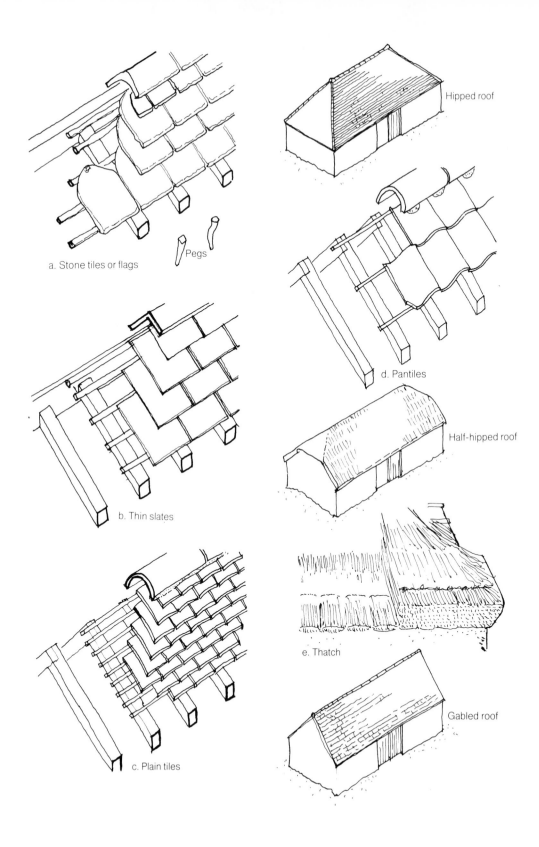

a. Stone tiles or flags

Pegs

b. Thin slates

c. Plain tiles

d. Pantiles

e. Thatch

Hipped roof

Half-hipped roof

Gabled roof

nineteenth centuries. In the north-eastern counties and in Somerset, pantiles were widely used on farm buildings over the same period. Finally, Welsh slates, waterborne by coastal shipping, river boat and canal barge, and eventually by railway wagon, came into widespread use, superseding all other materials, except tiles and pantiles. Many thatched buildings do survive, and some villages far from the spread of the railways remain fully thatched, but generally, the huge inventory of thatched farm buildings became fully slated during the nineteenth century. Only with the last decades of that century and during the decline of traditional methods of design as well as of construction did corrugated iron become the principal roofing material to be found on the farmstead.

In remote parts of northern and western Scotland both thatch and turf roof coverings remained in use long after they had been abandoned elsewhere. Turf was hung as 'divots', diamond set to low pitch. Thatch was often of heather or grass rather than straw, was renewed each year and was also laid to a low pitch but secured with the aid of coarse rope nets tied to stone weights or projecting blocks.

For some of the minor buildings of the farmstead, especially in the midland counties of England, the rafterless roof was employed. This consisted of a pile of brushwood or hedge clippings roughly made into the shape of a pitched roof and laid on a floor of branches which itself was usually carried by a crude timber framework of the type used in mud and stud construction. The roof-shaped pile was then thatched, and to outward appearance looked like any other thatched roof of narrow span.

Financing and constructional procedures
Responsibility for financing farm building construction varied considerably with time and place. In seventeenth century Scotland, for instance, the landlord provided a few pieces of timber and the tenant provided the rest and built the whole. In nineteenth century Staffordshire, on the other hand, the landlord provided the complete farmstead and the tenant paid an appropriate rent; this of course was the general pattern at that time and continues to the present day. The books of farm building plans circulated by hopeful architects from the mid-eighteenth century onwards often included quite detailed estimates of the cost of building to the designs in different materials and with variations according to what the prospective client could provide from his own quarries or timber yards.

Construction procedures varied similarly but attention now being paid to the estate account books, arriving in increasing quantities in the county record offices, is making the picture more clear and suggesting that in many cases procedures for contract and sub-contract were not so radically different from those employed at the present day.

106. Roof coverings.

Chapter 8

Recent developments and the re-use of farm buildings

Although the subject matter of this work is the design of traditional farm buildings and their grouping in farmsteads it would be wrong to conclude without some brief mention of the later farm buildings, aesthetically less appealing perhaps, which have been added to practically every single working farmstead in order to meet present day requirements. It is also important to consider the problem of the conservation of farm buildings, a problem which is acute because so few traditional farm buildings seem to serve any obvious purpose on the contemporary farmstead and urgent because so many traditional farm buildings are in an advanced state of structural decay.

From about 1880 to about 1940

The long years of agricultural depression were marked by a series of bad harvests at first, a great influx of cheap imported grain, a rather later but, if anything, more serious influx of cheap imported tinned meat, frozen meat and chilled meat and a political climate which would allow neither protection nor subsidy to the British farmer. For the landlord there were low rents from the farms which could still be let and poor profits from land which had to be taken in hand. Some land was sold to farmers who, as owner-occupiers, were often far too under-capitalised to invest in new buildings or maintain their existing stock. Most land still remained with landowners who had built up a practice of constructing and maintaining farm buildings in return for high rents, a practice which they could no longer afford to follow. Very few new farmsteads were built as little land was reclaimed or even re-organised, comparatively few new buildings were built, all the old buildings were inadequately maintained.

The existing stock of farm buildings was to some extent capable of adapting to the new emphasis on dairying – accommodation of dairy cattle had been part of the mixed farming organisation – but much of the plant was of substantial stone or brick and difficult to adapt to new ways of dairying and much was of timber-frame and weather-boarded construction too flimsy to adapt.

Nevertheless even during this period of depression there were developments in farm building design, some based on traditional practices and some preparing for the agricultural boom of the future.

On some of the largest East Anglian arable farms the combine harvester was introduced. This piece of equipment, developed in North America, cut and threshed the corn simultaneously in the field, but it was much more bulky than any of the other agricultural implements and the redundant barn was often the only place in which it could be housed. In the barn also went the grain drier which helped to make the grain harvested by the combine suitable for further processing.

Traditional cow-houses had long been condemned by the agricultural writers and legislation, particularly that of 1885 and 1926, made more and more stringent requirements for the hygiene in the cow-houses and for the greater comfort of the cattle. The traditional feeding passage with cows facing each other was virtually outlawed, as was the low dusty hay loft. Instead new cow-houses were single-storey and with longitudinal feeding passages, generously lit with windows in the walls and glazing in the roofs, tall, spacious and airy. At the same time increasingly severe hygiene regulations improved the design of the dairy and brought in the milk cooler and the provision for sterilisation by steam of the dairy utensils. Cow-house and dairy were linked, at first functionally and then literally, by the milking machine. The early milking machines, coming into use in the years just before the First World War, brought the milk from the udder into an enclosed bucket, but the cowman or milkmaid had still to carry the bucket across the farmyard to the dairy. Later milking machines, introduced just after the war, transferred the milk directly from udder to dairy through a system of pipes. The invention of the milking bail in the 1920s took the whole operation of milking from the cow-house to the field. A milking bail is a shed, on wheels, taken into the pastures and allowing cattle to be milked in groups of two or three in succession. This economical system could only be used on dry warm land; for other parts of the country the milking parlour was devised whereby cattle were milked in small batches on the farmstead near to the open or covered yard in which they were housed.

The Scandinavian piggery was further developed and farmers gradually began to understand the importance of insulation as well as heat in keeping the pigs happy and productive. Such piggeries were long, enclosed, blank-walled buildings as were the newly developed poultry houses designed for large-scale egg production.

Generally such new farm buildings as were erected in this period were scientifically designed for a specialised purpose or were designed for flexibility and adaptability. All continued to use brick and slate or tile, but steel frame and corrugated iron or asbestos was becoming more and more in evidence.

From about 1940 to the present day

Of necessity the great increase in agricultural production in Britain during the Second World War had to be accomplished using existing buildings and on existing farms. During the post-war period output has been maintained, and in many cases increased, from a constant area of farmland, using a decreasing labour force and with the aid of many new farm buildings. The period has been characterised by the influence of research on farming, including farm building design; the research has been done by Government agencies and by commercial firms selling farming equipment or farming aids, has built to a large extent on research done in other countries, and has been disseminated by way of governmental and commercial advisory services and applied with the aid of grants and subsidies.

The fruits of changed circumstances and substantial research have been enjoyed partly by way of new farm buildings. For the dairy cattle the distinction between the lying area and the milking area has been further developed: cattle continue to lie in yards where the climate permits but they are also housed in large sheds, similar in some ways to the covered yards of the nineteenth century but usually incorporating cubicles or stalls to which the cows wander at will. For milking the cattle are led to milking parlours and design has concentrated on minimising the labour for the cowman, maximising the number of cattle which a single man could milk while maintaining the highest levels of hygiene.

The storage and distribution of food for the cattle has changed radically. Hay is still made and bales of hay are still stored in Dutch barns, but the development of silage as fodder for cattle has made a big impact on farmstead design. Silage consists of grass cut green and short and kept in such conditions as prevents decay or over-heating. Previous spells of slight popularity of silage in the 1880s and early 1940s led to the construction of low rather squat towers for the storage of the grass, but nowadays the silage is made in huge half-subterranean pits and covered with polythene until grazed directly, but under control, by the cattle.

Silos of a different sort have added to the buildings of the farmstead. These tall domed towers contain grain and other fodder for the cattle and are sometimes connected to mechanical devices which transfer measured amounts of this food to the cattle.

Specialised buildings for pigs and poultry continue their development. The piggery is a long low shed, with controlled light and ventilation, heavily insulated and distinguished by its hopper at one end containing food which is fed automatically to the animals. The poultry shed is in many respects similar in appearance to the piggery; the poultry whether for egg production or as broilers are generally kept in tiers of battery cages and fed with Vitamin D rather than exposed to sunshine, though the deep litter system has been popular from time to time and free range poultry command a discerning market for their eggs.

The quantity of building on farms in the period since 1946 has been enormous, its architectural quality has brought much criticism. This is based both on overall design and proportions which lack either the traditional confidence of the older buildings or the ordered care of those of the mid and later nineteenth century and on building materials. These tend to be criticised either because they are flimsy materials put together on a do-it-yourself basis by the owner-occupier farmer or because they are garish materials (and sometimes flimsy also) prefabricated by manufacturers and erected without much thought for appropriate siting or for their impact on the rural landscape. However, associations of farmers and landowners as well as amenity bodies and national and local governmental organisations are increasingly aware of the value of good design and some very successful examples of good modern farm buildings have been publicised. Current problems relate both to new construction and to conservation of the existing stock, especially of traditional farm buildings.

Conservation and re-use of farm buildings
Traditional farm buildings provide a remarkable example of the way in which direct architectural response to simple functional requirements can produce happy and satisfying visual results. The barns, whether great storehouses for wealthy monasteries or utilitarian crop conversion plants on eighteenth-century family farms, possess a dignity (tempered sometimes by light touches of architectural playfulness) which the more sophisticated architecture of the

107. Hay barn of steel and corrugated sheeting, near Croft, Yorkshire This long building has a few bales of hay at one end, but the size indicates the capacity needed on farms which are now so highly productive.

present day finds impossible to capture. Indeed, traditional farm buildings, whatever their materials and constructional methods, carry an air of permanence which seems properly associated with the land they serve. Just as the pattern of field and hedgerow seems a permanent and unchanging part of the rural landscape, so the farm buildings seem an equally permanent, invulnerable, part of the rural architectural scene.

Yet we know that neither fields nor farm buildings are as invulnerable as they seem. Both are, in fact, part of a changing agricultural scene, one which is now changing swiftly after about a century of apparent stability. Field patterns are being modified, hedges grubbed up, stone walls thrown down because, in many counties, they no longer conform to modern methods of farming or to contemporary views on land holdings. Farm buildings are being abandoned, allowed to fall into ruin or demolished because they are obsolete in terms of present day farming practices. Hardly a single traditional farm building type can nowadays satisfactorily serve its original purpose. The barn for hand flail threshing, whether aisled or unaisled, has been obsolete for nearly two hundred years. The barn for machine threshing, whether designed for power by wind, water or horses, has been obsolete for nearly a hundred years. The barn for threshing powered by steam or oil engines has been obsolete for practically fifty years. Threshing itself, wherever carried out, has been obsolete for the twenty or thirty years since combine harvesters superseded the reaper/binder in our arable fields.

Cattle are rarely tied in cow-houses these days: if they are to be milked then it is virtually impossible to meet regulations on hygiene if they are housed in lofted cow-houses of traditional design. Since horses are very rarely used on farms nowadays the stables stand empty; if the farmer's daughter keeps a riding horse it is more likely that she will house it in a prefabricated wooden loose box than in a stable on the farmstead. Very few farmers or cottagers keep pigs and then not in the traditional pigsty; the few farmers who specialise in pig rearing have piggeries to serve as the barracks for their regiments of these animals.

Dovecots, where surviving, house a few decorative pigeons providing neither meat nor eggs nor manure. Poultry, if kept for sentimental reasons by the farmer's wife, are not kept in the dusty poultry loft over the empty pigsty but in a neat, clean, purpose-built shed.

Of the storage buildings, only the hay barn, itself a recent addition to the farmstead, plays much part in the modern farming economy, and even then it can only house the small proportion of grass which is made into hay and baled; the silage pit with its bleak polythene blanket and its congregation of motor car tyres holds the rest. The granary might contain a few sacks of grain from time to time, but the silo or hopper contains the bulk food for the animals and is a much more important part of the plant of the present day farmer. A large upland farm might have a hay or grain dryer but it would not resemble a traditional kiln in any particular. Few hop kilns are now used. Maltings have deserted the farmstead. Cartshed and other implement stores are too narrow and too low for modern machinery.

What applies to the individual farm building applies also to the collection of buildings on or off the farmstead. The bank barn may well lie empty since the barn has lost its sheaves long ago and its hay more recently; stable, cow-house

108. Hay barn of timber and corrugated sheeting, Llawr Llan, Breconshire Filled with bales of hay, this structure consists of timber posts (probably re-used telegraph poles) set in the ground and supporting a lightweight roof.

and cartshed down below have all lost their occupants. The Lancashire barn lies empty for the same reason. Field barns fall empty as fewer upland fields are cropped for hay and fewer farmers feel inclined to make the daily trudge, even by Land Rover, up the slopes.

The separate buildings of the farmstead and the farmyard itself have often been replaced by a single multi-purpose shed. Combining some of the characteristics of the foldyard, the cow-house, the shelter shed and the hay barn, such a shed gives freedom and shelter for the animals, is economical in food and litter and can be serviced by the farmer with minimum labour and maximum use of his tractor and other farm machinery.

So it is quite clear that since few traditional farm buildings are suitable for continued use in their original functions those which survive have either to be put to new uses on the farm or allowed to remain under-used, empty, or to fall into ruin. Any close examination of a typical farmstead shows that something of the sort has happened. Sometimes new farmsteads have been built alongside the old; sometimes the old buildings are lost in a mess of new additions and extensions of various ages, built in various materials and conforming to the styles of various manufacturers. Since new materials of asbestos-cement, painted steel and coloured aluminium are so different in every respect from the traditional, the new buildings do not sit in the same happy way with the old as eighteenth century brick additions sat happily with seventeenth century timber-frame.

Since the traditional farm buildings are increasingly recognised as a part of the national heritage, a part of the rural scene which is so highly prized, and since they are of social and historical interest as well as architectural, there is a growing movement for their preservation. This movement is to a surprisingly large extent understood and supported by farmers and landowners who are embarrassed by this substantial part of the national heritage which rests expensively and uselessly in their hands and for whose preservation to the present day they have carried the burden.

Some idea of the scale of this problem in building conservation may be seen if we take barns alone among farm building types. Statistics are available in part from 1875 and more completely from 1885, by which date the great wave of farm building construction in traditional manner had virtually come to an end. Taking 50 acres as the lowest limit for a family farm worked more or less as a full-time enterprise, there were in England and Wales, in 1885, 138,569 farms of that size or over and each one could reasonably be expected to have at least one barn. Even if as many as half of these barns have been demolished or altered out of recognition in the past 90 years or so then this still leaves a heritage of nearly 70,000 as potentially worth saving. A study of Essex barns estimated that more than 1400 barns had once existed in the county and that probably half of those survived in 1980. Studies have suggested that in Westmorland there were probably around 3,625 barns (a large proportion being bank barns) potentially of historical and architectural interest. Taking Essex as a representative county of large farms and large barns and Westmorland as one of small farms and barns then, again, a figure of 112,450 barns is suggested as the heritage in England and Wales and of that possibly 60,000 or so still survive. These are large numbers and should be considered with the total of about

109. Silo, near Abingdon, Oxfordshire The tall light-coloured feed storage silos are now a common sight in the countryside.

275,000 buildings which by 1981 had been 'listed' as being of architectural or historical importance and of which only a few are barns.

We have to accept that many farm buildings will have to be lost because their position makes the reorganisation of a farmstead for efficient operation impossible, or because they are already beyond economical repair, or because their architectural and historical interest is slight or has already been compromised. Those which are to survive will be chosen because they can be adapted to modern farming use, because they have been converted to other uses, because they have been preserved as museums or because they have been transferred and re-assembled in national or regional folk museums.

The strongest candidates for continued farm use are probably the largest barns, including the large aisled barns. Given end entry rather than side entry and making use of fork-lift trucks and palleted loads such buildings can be made to provide dry and well-ventilated storage for crops, produce, fodder and fertilisers. Their maintenance is not cheap but their modification for new farming use may not be expensive and need not seriously affect their appearance or interest as farm buildings.

Large barns, including aisled barns, are also probably the best candidates for use by the public as museums, assembly halls of various sorts, libraries etc. Unlike most buildings of architectural or historic interest barns do not have windows as an essential element in their design and so lend themselves to activities which require windowless buildings. Museum use falls in that category and the Fox Talbot Museum of Photography at Lacock in Wiltshire is an example of successful adaptation. Since barns have a long history of use for assembly when empty, a history represented by the term 'barn dance', by associations with nonconformist and evangelical religious movements and by passages in novels about country life such as *Far from the Madding Crowd*, large barns can be made into assembly halls or village halls without too much loss of character. The Tithe Barn at Harrow, Middlesex, for instance has been made into a sort of village hall and that in Rickmansworth into a school assembly hall.

Conversion of barns to restaurant use has quite a long history. One of the earliest examples and still one of the best is the cruck-framed Hall Barn at Rivington, Lancashire which was made into a refreshment room by William Hesketh Lever, first Lord Leverhulme, in 1911 for the benefit of the local industrial workers visiting the park he had established on the slopes of Rivington Pike. This vast and powerful structure can accommodate a children's birthday party, a women's club sitting down to a set tea, a group of motor cyclists bound for Blackpool and any number of family groups pausing while on a visit to the park, all at the same time and all without any one group appearing to intrude on any other.

There have been some very successful instances of the conversion of farm buildings into arts and crafts and general social centres. One well-known instance is the Fiddick Farm Centre in Washington New Town, County Durham where a range of stone-walled farm buildings remaining from a very large farm have been adapted to these new uses and at the same time provide an important element of historical and architectural continuity in this largely modern and artificial creation of a new town. Another well-known instance on a smaller scale is the Lains Barn Centre at Wantage, Berkshire where local initiative and a high proportion of local labour have converted a redundant farmstead into a very active social centre.

Farm buildings are also being developed for holiday use. One way is to organise farmhouse holidays, as has been done so successfully in Denmark; the

110. Farming musuem, Cogges, Witney, Oxfordshire A great variety of building types and building materials may be seen in this farmstead now open to the public as a museum of farming, farm implements and farm buildings.

farming activity becomes part of the holiday attraction, especially for young children, and adaptation of some buildings for holiday use while retaining other buildings for some part or complete farming use makes the total farmstead once more an intricate organisation of interlocking uses. Another sort of holiday use comes of the conversion of buildings into holiday houses and flats; by this means the dispersion of cars and service lines which might litter the countryside is avoided. Yet another sort of holiday use has recently been the subject of experiments both in the Yorkshire Dales and the Peak District: small redundant farm buildings such as field barns have been converted into 'stone tents' providing limited overnight accommodation for hikers; such conversions provide shelter more appealing than a tent but less elaborate even than a youth hostel.

Both single farm buildings and complete farmsteads can be made into museums of farming. Popular and architecturally successful examples include the Home Farm at Beamish, County Durham and Cogges Farm at Witney, Oxfordshire. Interest is tending to move towards such comprehensive folk museums which can show on one site (and an authentic site at that) the separate activities of domestic life at various social levels and farming from the growing of traditional crops, some long-abandoned, cultivated by traditional processes, to the tending of traditional breeds of animals. But there are still strong arguments for the development of national or regional museums of re-erected buildings on the lines pioneered at Skansen in Stockholm and best represented in Britain by the Welsh Folk Museum at St. Fagans and in England by such examples as the Weald and Downland Museum, the Avoncroft Museum and the Stowmarket Museum. All these and the Ulster Folk Museum include re-erected farm buildings.

However, the greatest demand for redundant farm buildings is for conversion to domestic use. Here the large structures such as the aisled barns are the least adaptable whereas smaller barns, especially stone-walled, with plenty of pitching holes to turn into windows, are in much demand in certain areas. There are problems especially in the introduction of bathrooms and kitchens, but, month by month, the magazines show examples which have been quite successful. Even apparently unpromising subjects such as circular oast houses have led to successful conversion.

Although so many successful examples of the conversion of farm buildings to new uses may be found, it would be wrong to imagine that the problem is easily solved or that many of the accepted solutions have proved entirely successful. There are questions of conservation philosophy to be asked, consideration of planning policy to be made, there are the attitudes of various regulatory bodies to be acknowledged, all apart from the basic economics of conversion and re-use.

The main question in conservation philosophy is the extent to which farm buildings lose in conversion the very characteristics which justified their preservation in the first place. This is a problem in all attempts at historic preservation of buildings through re-use, but it seems to be a particularly severe problem in relation to farm buildings since the connection between use and architectural expression in their original design is so direct. Yet it is often the bulk, the silhouette, the overall proportions of farm buildings which matter from a distance and the colour and texture of their constructional materials which matter at close approach. Such powerful buildings can often master the external changes needed for re-use and even, sometimes, the internal alterations without loss of distinctive character as former farm buildings.

Planning policy relates partly to the location of farm buildings as candidates for conversion and re-use. A farmstead in a village has potential for conversion into a village hall, a field barn near the Pennine Way has potential for conversion into a 'stone tent'. But farm buildings are obsolete and redundant everywhere: in Herefordshire or Shropshire or Lincolnshire as much as in Buckinghamshire or Westmorland or the Cotswolds. It is difficult, whatever the planning policy, to think of alternative uses for farm buildings which are too far from big cities to serve as permanent homes, too far from the popular tourist

111. Oast house conversion near Staple Cross, Sussex Many oast houses have been converted to domestic use without concealing their original farming purpose.

areas to serve as holiday accommodation or second homes, too strongly linked to depopulated rural areas to justify commercial, industrial or community use, and too remote from busy roads and adequate services to function as museums. Yet these farm buildings might have served farming areas which have always been important and which have produced the most valuable agricultural architecture. There are areas, often of small population and low rateable value, with strong claims for special planning consideration and for special outside help.

Planning policy sometimes has an unhelpful effect when applied in districts where demand for farm buildings for conversion and re-use is high. A farmer or landowner might complain that he is anxious to convert redundant farm buildings into holiday houses or lettable workshops but is frustrated by planning policies which discourage such use. A planner, on the other hand, might complain that the countryside would not be preserved if every redundant farm building were put to a new use which created traffic congestion, noise or smoke, overloading of services and so on. A barn is no longer a barn if it has cable for three-phase electricity spoiling its silhouette and half-completed vehicles or empty packing cases littering its plan; a field barn is no longer a field barn if lights are shining from inside and washing is flapping on a line outside. Arguments on planning policy are especially contentious in National Parks where farm buildings are so important a part of the landscape which justified designation in the first place, where obsolescence and redundancy for farming purposes are just as likely as elsewhere, where demands for holiday accommodation are so strong and yet where balance of uses is so delicate if total character is to be maintained.

Other regulatory and advisory bodies sometimes find it difficult to come to terms with the re-use of farm buildings. There are limits to the extent to which government aid to farming can be directed to adaptation and re-use rather than demolition and new construction. Building regulations based on the protection of the health and safety of the public in normal circumstances may seem excessively severe when applied, say, to conversion of farm buildings for holiday use. Food and hygiene regulations, admirable in themselves, may seem to be applied with excessive enthusiasm when small numbers of hikers 'getting away from it all' are the ones to be protected.

The economics of conversion and re-use are rarely simple. On the face of it there will be many cases, perhaps most, in which demolition and rebuilding on a new site may appear more economical in the narrowest accounting terms than adaptation or rehabilitation. Yet other factors should be allowed to broaden the calculations: the actual cost of rebuilding in traditional materials, for instance, or the American concept of total energy cost whereby the value of energy already consumed in producing the existing buildings should be set in the accounting balance.

Conclusion

In spite of the economic distortions of the Common Market it seems likely, perhaps inevitable, that a large proportion of the food that can be grown in Britain for its population will continue to be grown here. A farming labour force which seems unlikely to increase will have to continue its task on farms which become steadily more efficient and which use such buildings as are thought necessary in a steadily more economical way. Few traditional farm buildings have traditional roles to fulfil, few can satisfactorily meet present day farming requirements. Many are long past their structural life, nearly all are expensive to maintain. Some at least, perhaps many, will inevitably be lost. More ingenuity, more care, and more incentives could make more of the traditional buildings useful to the present day farmer. More ingenuity, more flexibility on the part of regulatory bodies could surely enable many traditional buildings to be converted to new uses. All these pieces of conservation work depend, or are at least considerably aided, by an understanding of the buildings themselves, of the processes they were designed to accommodate, of the choice of building materials and constructional systems that were made. This understanding can only follow a greater and greater effort towards the recording and study of farm buildings while they are still with us in very substantial quantities. Such efforts depend on a climate of public opinion receptive to the idea that farm buildings are not mere sheds and boxes but buildings worth study in their own right. It is encouraging that more and more signs suggest that this climate of public opinion is forming and that study will indeed take place before it is too late.

Notes and references

General note on references and recommendations for further reading.

1. References are to the Select Bibliography, thus 'N. W. Alcock (1982)' refers to N. W. Alcock, *Cruck Construction: an Introduction and Catalogue*, 1982.

2. Farm buildings in their farming background
a. generally: Hoskins (1955) provides the best-known general introduction to the landscape, including farming and farm buildings; Higgs (1964) gives a clear and concise introduction to farming history.
b. Among the observant travellers, the best-known in reference to farming and farm buildings are Defoe (edn. of 1971) and Cobbett (edn. of 1967).
c. Contemporary regional impressions of agriculture may be gleaned from the Reports to the Board of Agriculture. These were submitted mostly during the 1790s; under a series of headings they were intended to give a comprehensive description of the state of agriculture in England and Wales at the time; for many counties there were revisions of the original report and then a second edition in the early nineteenth century. The reports were entitled *General View of the Agriculture of. . .* e.g. Bailey & Culley (1805) and this and several others have recently been re-issued. A *Review and Abstract* of the county reports was prepared by W. Marshall in 1808–18. Arthur Young published his observations on agricultural conditions based on tours in the late eighteenth century. In the early volumes of the *Journal of the Royal Agricultural Society for England* there were published Prize Reports on the state of agriculture in the counties about the middle of the nineteenth century. A survey region by region in 1851–2 was made by J. Caird (edn. of 1968).

3. Farm building design
a. Starting in the eighteenth century but mostly during the nineteenth century there were books on farm building design, usually incorporating some recommended layouts. One of the first is Garrett (1747) another fairly early is Lugar (1807) but the best-known are Dean (1849), Denton (1863), Henderson (1902), Lawrence (1919), Loudon (1835 & '36), Stephens (1854 & '61) and Waistell (1827).

b. Of recent books on the history of farm buildings the principal are the following: Peters and Darley (1981) and Harvey (1970 and 1980) for England as a whole, Peters (1969) for Staffordshire, a county of well organised mixed farming, William (1982) for a part of North Wales with a variety of farming practices, and Fenton & Walker (1981) for Scottish farm buildings.
c. Unpublished theses on farm buildings include the following: L. Caffyn (1981) an MA (Method I) dissertation on farm buildings in parts of Sussex, D. C. G. Davies (1952) a pioneering MA thesis on farm buildings in part of Shropshire; these two are in the University of Manchester as are the theses from which the books by Peters (1969) and Wiliam (1982) developed. In the University of York is the Conservation Studies Diploma dissertation *Farm Buildings: Function and Form* of J. Popham (1973). In the University of East Anglia is the PhD Dissertation of S. Wade-Martins on the *Holkham Estate*, including farm buildings, though of a planned rather than a traditional nature (1975).

4. Bibliographies
Apart from the select bibliography here, and the bibliographies contained in the various books listed in it, there are references to traditional farm buildings in Sir Robert Hall (ed.) *A Bibliography on Vernacular Architecture* (1972) and the supplements to be issued by the Vernacular Architecture Group of which the first is D. J. H. Michelmore *A Current Bibliography of Vernacular Architecture*, Vol. 1 1970–76 (1979).

5. Periodicals
The following include occasional articles on traditional farm buildings
Agricultural History Review
Country Life
Folk Life: the Journal of the Society for Folk Life Studies
Industrial Archaeology
Industrial Archaeology Review
Journal of the Royal Agricultural Society of England
Journals of the Society of Architectural Historians (UK and USA separately)
Medieval Archaeology
Post-Medieval Archaeology
Transactions of the Ancient Monuments Society

Vernacular Architecture: the Journal of the Vernacular Architecture Group.

In addition, the transactions of the various county archaeological societies include relevant articles from time to time.

6. Museums

Many museums include libraries, archives etc. as well as collections of objects related to farm buildings and their use. Among the principal national museums related to agriculture are:

Museum of English Rural Life, Reading, Berks.
Welsh Folk Museum. St. Fagans, Cardiff
National Museum of Antiquities of Scotland, Edinburgh

Chapter 1 **Farming history**

General: immediate sources are Chambers and Mingay (1966), Ernle (1936), Kerridge (1967 and 1973); in addition, of the projected Agrarian History of England and Wales, Vol IV covering the period 1500–1640 has appeared, Thirsk (1967).

Medieval to c 1350: Beresford & St. Joseph (1979) is helpful.

1350–1560 and 1560–1750: Thirsk (1967) is relevant here, including Welsh material by F. V. Emery; Fussell and Atwater (1936) provides an early instance for the appreciation of the value of probate inventories in the study.

1750–1850: typical leases requiring the farmers to see that all the crops were consumed on the farm to produce manure were quoted in Tuke (1794), p. 22; Rennie, Brown and Shirreff (1794) p. 10 comment on the practice of the Yorkshire 'manufacturers' leaving their looms for the fields at harvest time.

Scottish material: based mainly on Fenton (1976), Fenton and Walker (1981) and Millman (1975).

Chapter 2 **Barns and the Processing of grain crops**

General: Fussell (1952), Jewell (1975), and Partridge (1973) provide background and illustrations of the various items of tools and machinery used in the barn.

Tithe barns: examples and data principally from Andrews (1900), Charles and Horn (1973), Horn (1963), Horn and Born (1965), Horn and Charles (1966); the oldest dated monastic tithe barn is believed to be that of Church Enstone belonging to the Abbey of Winchcombe, datestone 1382, see Wood-Jones, (1963) p. 15.

Barns for hand flail threshing

The practice of threshing in the open air was perpetuated in Ryedale, Yorkshire, in the late eighteenth century, see Tuke (1794) p. 38. Practice of threshing by beating a sheaf on a partition survived until the twentieth century,

Hartley and Ingleby (1972) p. 64. Practice of hand flail threshing survived into the twentieth century, Hartley and Ingleby (1972) p. 67, also personal communication E. Atkinson, 1980. Threshing floors of earth and oxblood: Partridge (1973) p. 161, and of cast iron, Smedley (1976) pp. 89–91. Ways to relieve the monotony of hand flail threshing described in G. E. Evans, (1956) p. 95. 'Riding the goaf' described by G. E. Evans, (1969) p. 83. The owl hole was introduced following a plague of rats in 1730, see E. L. Jones, 'The Bird Pests of British Agriculture in Recent Centuries', *Agricultural History Review*, 1972, p. 115, quoted in Harvey (1980) p. 136. The corn hole is illustrated in Harris (1979), (reproducing a drawing from *Communications to the Board of Agriculture, 1797*) p. 13; the feature seems to have been particularly popular in Staffordshire and Suffolk, Peters (1969) pp. 97–8 and Peters (1981) pp. 17–18. The rate of work at threshing is quoted in Vancouver (1808) p. 148. For introduction of winnowing machine see Fussell (1952), pp. 158–9.

Aisled barns

The analogy with church design was made as early as 1794: 'large barns we saw at several places which are more like churches than barns', Rennie, Brown and Shirreff, (1794) p. 73. For medieval references to aisled barn design and for their late use see Rigold (1967). For distribution of aisled barns see Rigold (1971), Clarke (1973) and Ryder (1981) pp. 382–5. The analogy with hall-like buildings generally is developed in Horn (1958) and Horn and Born (1968).

Barns for machine threshing

Developments are traced in Fussell (1952) pp. 152–7, Partridge (1973) pp. 161–5, Macdonald (1975) pp. 63–7, and (1978) pp. 168–73. Use of Horse-engine traced in Atkinson (1960–1) pp. 31–5, Macdonald (1978) pp. 177–81 and (1975), Fenton and Walker (1981) pp. 160–1. Rate of adoption and distribution of examples detailed in Hutton (1976), Hellen (1972) pp. 140–54, Fox (1978) and Macdonald (1975). Smaller versions of horse-engine mentioned in Partridge (1973) pp. 203–4, Hartley and Ingleby (1972) p. 69, Fenton and Walker (1981) pp. 167–80.

Mixing house barn

The books of farm building design of later nineteenth century and early twentieth century took the threshing machine and its steam power as the basis for planning e.g. Stephens (1861), Denton (1864), Henderson (1902).

Chapter 3 **Accommodation for animals**

General: The term 'cattle' is used here to mean cows, bulls, oxen, heifers and bullocks. The term is less consistently used in older books and documents when cattle can also mean horses.

Cow-houses

The general reference is Fussell (1966) pp. 136–46. Some idea of traditional practices in wintering cattle may be gained from modern practice explained in Grundy (1970), pp. 3–5. Space allocated to cattle has increased from about 2 ft. 3 ins (685 mm) at Black Daren, a late medieval house in Herefordshire, through 2 ft. 6 ins (762 mm) at Cilewent, *c.* 1730 re-erected at the Welsh Folk Museum and 3 ft 6 ins (1.06 m) per cow in double stalls recommended in Lawrence (1919) to 4 ft. (1.22 mm) per cow in single stalls recommended in Ministry of Agriculture (1945).

Farmyards and foldyards

Grundy (1970) p. 3 points out that even now yard housing is concentrated in eastern arable areas where plenty of straw is available.

Shelter sheds

There are various other terms such as 'cowshed', 'hovel', 'helm' used for what is here called a shelter shed. For more information on linhays see Alcock (1963) pp. 117–26; the word is also used generally in Devon and Cornwall for a lean-to building. Economy of straw noted in Lawrence (1919) pp. 7–8 and Peters (1969) p. 140.

Stables

G. E. Evans (1969) gives a rule of thumb of one horse to each 20 to 25 acres of arable land on a farm.

Pigsties

For circular pigsties see Wiliam (1980).

Chapter 4 Accommodation for birds

Dovecots

The seventeenth century estimate is quoted in Briggs (1953) p. 56. Vancouver (1808) includes a tirade about pigeons generally, including an estimate of 1,125,000 pairs of such birds in England and Wales.

Chapter 5 Granaries and storage and conversion of crops

For granaries on staddle stones see Harding (1976) pp. 94–5 and also *Guide to Weald and Downland Museum* pp. 35–9.

Corn drying kilns

Williams (1972) pp. 101–3 describes and illustrates a domestic kiln; Fenton and Walker (1981) pp. 32, 138, 164, 167–8 describe Scottish provision; G. Beresford (1979) pp. 140–42 describes kilns used in deteriorating medieval climate on Dartmoor.

Oast houses

Loudon (1836) pp. 595–9 describes the process; Homes (1978) pp. 12–16 relates it to Herefordshire and Worcestershire; Harvey (1980) p. 147 refers to surveys of oast houses in Kent; Y. T. Yong in Wade (1980) pp. 12–15 describes and illustrates an example dated 1815 in Kent.

Maltings

Lugar (1807) p. 25 describes the process and illustrates a typical small maltings.

Haybarns

A haybarn with an adjustable roof was suggested by Sir Hugh Plat in the early seventeenth century according to Fussell (1966) p. 124; also described and recommended in Vancouver (1808) p. 128 'said to have been borrowed from the Dutch . . .' but also widely used in the USA to protect both corn and hay.

Chapter 6 Farmsteads

Longhouses, laithe-houses and bastle houses

For longhouses Mercer (1975) Chapter III and P. Smith (1975) pp. 144–5 and pp. 159–61 provide a starting point for the quite extensive literature; for laithe-houses the main reference is Stell (1965) p. 20 where the term is coined from a Yorkshire word for a barn; for bastle houses the main reference is Ramm, McDowall and Mercer (1970), the term has become accepted though it was loosely used in the past; a late version of the bastle house arrangement appears in Atkinson (1977) p. 57.

Lancashire Barns

The building type was first identified by Mrs. J. Grundy in talks to the Vernacular Architecture Group.

Bank barn

The building type was recognized by Walton (1956) and described by McDowall (1956) p. 133; it had been illustrated but not named in Lawrence (1919) pp. 30–32; I described and illustrated the building in Brunskill (1970) pp. 138–9, giving it the American name which has now been generally adopted in this country. A contemporary plan of a bank barn is reproduced in Messenger (1975) p. 337. The Pennsylvania Barn was given its German origin by Learned (1915); recent investigation into sources has been by Ensminger (1980) and Jordan (1980).

Field barns and outfarms

Further described and illustrated in Brunskill (1976) pp. 127–9; use explained in Harley and Ingleby (1968) pp. 29–35; described and approved for economy of labour by Tuke (1794); in Willan and Croseley (1941) it appears from a survey of the manor of Wensleydale in 1613 that of 102 houses, 23 had fieldhouses, some two or three giving a total of 38 fieldhouses, proof of use before the main enclosures.

Chapter 7 Materials and Construction

Most forms of construction are common to domestic and farm buildings and the subject is further developed in Brunskill (1970 and 1978), and Clifton-Taylor (1972) and was pioneered by Innocent (1916 and 1972). Timber-frame construction generally is introduced in

Harris (1978). Matters of cruck construction are developed in Alcock (1982) and Charles and Horn (1973); and of box-frame and post-and-truss construction in Hewett (1980). Examples of financing and constructional procedures for farm buildings may be seen in Tyson (1979, 80, 81). Scottish material is summarised in Fenton and Walker (1981).

Chapter 8 Recent developments and the re-use of farm buildings

Recent developments
Main sources are Harvey (1970), Ministry of Agriculture (1945 and 1968), and Weller (1965).
Conservation and re-use of farm buildings
The matter is briefly considered in the Montagu Report (1980) pp. 5, 6, 24–9. Figures for barns are based on Ministry of Agriculture (1968), Essex County Council (1980), Davies (1980). The 'stone tents' experiment is recounted in Countryside Commission (1980) and in a Derbyshire County Council feasibility study.
Farmsteads open to the public
Although most farms and farmsteads are private and not normally open to the public, there are, in fact many ways in which farm buildings may be visited. The annual lists published by the Automobile Association, *Britain's Heritage*, and by ABC Historic Publications, *Historic Houses, Castles and Gardens*, and *Museums and Galleries* include many farm buildings.
1. The *National Trust* owns many farm buildings which are open under their usual arrangements e.g Great Coxwell Tithe Barn, Oxfordshire, East Riddlesden Hall Barn, Yorkshire, and a dozen dovecots. Particulars appear in the annual *Properties open . . . essential information for Visitors.*

2. *Department of the Environment* has some farm buildings in care e.g. Bradford on Avon Tithe Barn, Wiltshire, open like other Ancient Monuments.
3. *Historic Buildings Councils* for England, Wales and Scotland, recommend to the Secretary of State for the Environment buildings to receive grants in aid of repairs, some of these are farm buildings, and normally reasonable public access is a condition of aid. Particulars of some of these buildings appear in the annual lists of the AA and ABC Publications.
4. *Farming Museums* are usually located in farm buildings; among the best known are the Acton Scott Museum in Shropshire, the Cogges Museum at Witney in Oxfordshire, and the Beamish Open Air Museum in County Durham. Particulars are in the AA and ABC Publications mentioned and in S. Toulson, *Discovering Farm Museums and Farm Parks*, 1977.
5. *Museums of Re-erected Buildings* include some farm buildings; among the most developed are the Weald and Downland Museum at West Dean, Singleton, Sussex, the Museum of East Anglian Rural Life at Stowmarket in Suffolk, the Avoncroft Museum of Buildings at Bromsgrove in Worcestershire, and the Welsh Folk Museum at St. Fagans, Cardiff.
6. *Farming Open Days* give an opportunity to visit farms. They vary in frequency from place to place and time to time, but the various Tourist Boards often provide particulars in Tourist Information Centres.
7. *Farmhouse Holidays* can also provide opportunities to explore farm buildings, especially where the farm is advertised as one of the attractions in the holiday. Many lists of such holidays are produced and are available in bookshops and Tourist Information Centres.

Select bibliography

Agriculture, Ministry of, *A Century of Agricultural Statistics 1866–1966*, 1968

Agriculture, Ministry of, *Farm Buildings, Post War Buildings Studies No. 17*, 1945

N. W. Alcock, 'Devonshire Linhays', *Transactions of the Devonshire Association*, Vol. XCV, 1963

N. W. Alcock, *Cruck Construction: an Introduction and Catalogue*, 1982

F. W. B. Andrews, 'Medieval Tithe Barns', *Transactions of the Birmingham Archaeology Society*, Vol. XXIV, for 1899 (published 1900)

F. Atkinson, 'The Horse as a source of Rotary Power', *Transactions of The Newcomen Society*, Vol. XXXIII, 1960–1

F. Atkinson, *Life and Tradition in Northumberland and Durham*, 1977

D. C. Bailey and M. C. Tindall, 'Dovecots of East Lothian', *Transactions of the Ancient Monuments Society*, NS, Vol. 11, 1963

J. Bailey and G. Culley, *General View of the Agriculture of Northumberland, Cumberland and Westmorland*, 1972 facsimile of the 1805 edition

A. R. H. Baker and J. B. Harley, *Man Made the Land*, 1973

W. G. Benoy, *Farm Buildings: Conversions and Improvements*, 1956

G. Beresford, 'Three Deserted Medieval Settlements on Dartmoor', *Medieval Archaeology*, Vol. 23, 1979

M. W. Beresford and J. K. St. Joseph, *Medieval England*, 2nd. ed., 1979

M. S. Briggs, *The English Farmhouse*, 1953

H. Brooksby, 'Houses of Radnorshire, Pt. VI', *Radnorshire Society Transactions*, 1973

F. E. Brown, 'Aisled Timber Barns in East Kent', *Vernacular Architecture*, Vol. 7, 1976

H. Brunner and J. K. Major, 'Water Raising by Animal Power', *Industrial Archaeology*, Vol. 9 No. 2, May 1972

R. W. Brunskill, 'The Development of the Small House in the Eden Valley, from 1650 to 1840', *Transactions of the Cumberland and Westmorland Antiquarian and Archaeological Society*, NS, Vol. LIII, 1953

R. W. Brunskill, *Design and Layout of Farmsteads in Parts of Cumberland and Westmorland*, typescript Neale Bursary Report, RIBA Library, 1965.

R. W. Brunskill, *Illustrated Handbook of Vernacular Architecture*, 1970, 2nd ed., 1978

R. W. Brunskill, *Vernacular Architecture of the Lake Counties*, 1974

R. W Brunskill, 'Recording the Buildings of the Farmstead', *Transactions of the Ancient Monuments Society*, NS, Vol. 21, 1975–6

R. W. Brunskill, 'Vernacular Architecture of the Northern Pennines: a Preliminary View', *Northern History*, Vol. XI, 1976

A. H. Burges, *Hops*, 1964

J. Caird, *English Agriculture in 1850–51*, 1968 re-issue of 1852 ed.

J. D. Chambers and G. E. Mingay, *The Agricultural Revolution 1750–1880*, 1966

F. W. B. Charles and W. Horn, 'The Cruck-Built Barn of Leigh Court, Worcs.' *Journal of the Society of Architectural Historians* (USA), Vol. 32, 1973

D. W. Clarke, 'Pennine Aisled Barns', *Vernacular Architecture*, Vol. 4, 1973

A. Clifton-Taylor, *The Pattern of English Building*, 2nd ed., 1972

W. Cobbett, *Rural Rides*, 1830 (edn. of 1967)

Countryside Commission for England, *Bunk House Barns*, CCP 131, 1978

G. Darley, *The National Trust Book of the Farm*, 1981

N. W. I. Davies, *Barns and Barn Conversions in Cumbria*, report, Dept. of Building Technology, Brunel University, 1980

G. A. Dean, *Essays on the Construction of Farm Buildings and Labourers' Cottages*, 1849

D. Defoe, *A Tour Through the Whole Island of Great Britain, 1724–6*, ed. of 1971

J. B. Denton, *The Farm Homesteads of England*, 1864

Design Council, *Catalogue of Farm Buildings*, 1977

C. H. Dornbusch and J. K. Heyl, 'Pennsylvania German Barns', *Pennsylvania German Folklore Society*, (Allentown Pa., USA) Vol. 21, 1956

D. Dymond, 'A fifteenth century Building Contract from Suffolk', *Vernacular Architecture*, Vol. 9, 1978

S. Ebbage, *Barns and Granaries in Norfolk*, 1976

R. F. Ensminger, 'A Search for the Origins of the Pennsylvania Barn', *Pennsylvania Folklife*, Vol. XXX No. 2, 1980

Lord Ernle (R. E. Prothero), *English Farming, Past and Present*, 1912, (edn. of 1936)

Essex County Council Planning Department, *The Essex Countryside: Historic Barns*, 1980

G. E. Evans, *Ask The Fellows Who Cut the Hay*, 1956

G. E. Evans, *The Farm and the Village*, 1969

G. E. Evans, *The Pattern under the Plough*, 1966

A. Fenton, *Scottish Country Life*, 1976

A. Fenton and B. Walker, *The Rural Architecture of Scotland*, 1981

N. E. Fox, 'The Spread of the Threshing Machine in Central Southern England', *Agricultural History Review*, 1978

G. E. Fussell, *The Farmer's Tools, 1500–1900*, 1952

G. E. Fussell, *The English Dairy Farmer, 1500–1900*, 1966

G. E. Fussell, and U. H. B. Atwater, 'Farmer's Goods and Chattels, 1500 to 1800', *History*, Vol. XX, 1936

D. Garrett, *Design & Estimates of Farmhouses for the County of York etc.*, 1747

J. Grey, 'On Farm Buildings', *Journal of the Royal Agricultural Society of England*, Vol. IV, 1843, p. 117

J. E. Grundy, 'Notes on the relationship between climate and cattle housing', *Vernacular Architecture*, Vol. I, 1970

J. M. Harding, *Four Centuries of Charlwood Houses*, 1976

R. Harris, *Discovering Timber-Framed Buildings*, 1978

R. Harris, *Traditional Farm Buildings*, Catalogue to Arts Council Touring Exhibition, 1979

M. Hartley and J. Ingleby, *Life and Tradition in the Yorkshire Dales*, 1968

M. Hartley and J. Ingleby, *Life and Tradition in the Moorlands of North-East Yorkshire*, 1972

N. Harvey, *A History of Farm Buildings in England and Wales*, 1970

N. Harvey, *The Industrial Archaeology of Farming in England and Wales*, 1980

R. Henderson, *The Modern Homestead*, 1902

C. A. Hewett, *English Historic Carpentry*, 1980

J. Higgs, *The Land*, 1964

I. Homes, 'The Agricultural Use of the Herefordshire House and its Outbuildings', *Vernacular Architecture*, Vol. 9, 1978

W. Horn, 'On the Origins of the Medieval Bay System', *Journal of the Society of Architectural Historians* (USA), Vol. XVII, 1958

W. Horn, 'The Great Tithe Barn of Cholsey, Berkshire', *Journal of the Society of Architectural Historians* (USA), Vol. XXII, 1963

W. Horn and E. Born, *The Barns of the Abbey of Beaulieu At its Granges of Great Coxwell and Beaulieu St Leonard's*, 1965

W. Horn and F. W. B. Charles, 'The Cruck-Built Barn of Middle Littleton, Worcestershire', *Journal of the Society of Architectural Historians* (USA) Vol. XXV, 1966

W. G. Hoskins, *The Making of the English Landscape*, 1955

C. Howard, *General View of the Agriculture of the East Riding of Yorkshire*, 1835

J. Hume, 'Scottish Windmills, A Preservation Policy', Scottish Vernacular Architecture Working Group, *Newsletter*, no. 5, 1979

B. Hutton (ed.), *Hatfield and Its People*, Book 9, 1962

C. F. Innocent, *The Development of English Building Construction*, 1916 (edn. of 1972)

M. G. Jarrett and S. Wrathmell, 'Sixteenth and Seventeenth Century Farmsteads: West Whelpington, Northumberland', *Agricultural History Review*, Vol. 25, 1977

C. A. Jewell (ed.), *Victorian Farming – A Source Book*, 1975

D. H. Jones & J. K. Major, 'Drying Kilns attached to British Corn Mills', *Report of International Molinological Society, 3rd Symposium*, 1973

T. G. Jordan, 'Alpine, Alemannic and American Log Architecture', *Annals of the Association of American Geographers*, Vol. 70, no. 2, 1980

E. Kerridge, *The Agricultural Revolution*, 1967

E. Kerridge, *The Farmers of Old England*, 1973

C. P. Lawrence, *Economic Farm Buildings*, 1919

M. D. Learned, 'The German Barn in America', *University of Pennsylvania Lectures, 1913–1914*, (Philadelphia, Penna., USA) 1915

P. Leith and S. Spence, 'Orkney Threshing Mills', Scottish Vernacular Building Working Group, *Newsletter* No. 3, 1977

J. C. Loudon, *An Encyclopedia of Agriculture*, 3rd ed., 1835

J. C. Loudon, *An Encyclopedia of Cottage, Villa and Farm Architecture*, 1836

R. Lugar, *The Country Gentleman's Architect*, 1807

S. Macdonald, 'The Early Threshing Machine in Northumberland', *Tools and Tillage*, Vol. III, No. 3, 1978

S. Macdonald, 'The Progress of the Early Threshing Machine', *Agricultural History Review*, 1975 and 1978

S. Macdonald, 'Model Farms', Chapter 16 in G. E. Mingay (ed.) *The Victorian Countryside*, 1981

R. McDowall, 'The Westmorland Vernacular', in W. A. Singleton (ed.) *Studies in Architectural History*, Vol. II, 1956

W. Marshall, *The Rural Economy of Yorkshire*, 1788

R. N. Millman, *The Making of the Scottish Landscape*, 1975

A. J. Massingham, *The English Countryman*, 1942

D. Mercer, 'Roomed and Roomless Grain-Drying Kilns: the Hebridean Boundary', *Transactions of the Ancient Monuments Society*, NS, Vol. 19, 1972

E. Mercer, *English Vernacular Houses*, 1975

P. Messenger, 'Lowther Farmstead Plans: A Preliminary View', *Transactions of the Cumberland and Westmorland Antiquarian and Archaeological Society*, NS, Vol. 75, 1975

Lord Montagu, (Chairman), *Britain's Historic Buildings: a Policy for their Future Use*, 1980

M. Partridge, *Farm Tools Through the Ages*, 1973

J. E. C. Peters, 'The Tithe Barn, Arreton, Isle of Wight', *Transactions of the Ancient Monuments Society*, NS, Vol. 12, 1964

J. E. C. Peters, *The Development of Farm Buildings in Western Lowland Staffordshire up to 1880*, 1969

J. E. C. Peters, 'The Solid Thatch Roof', *Vernacular*

Architecture, Vol. 8, 1977

J. E. C. Peters, 'The Wall as a Truss in Farm Buildings', *Vernacular Architecture*, Vol. 11, 1980

J. E. C. Peters, *Discovering Traditional Farm Buildings*, 1981

D. Portman, 'Vernacular Buildings in the Oxford Region in the Sixteenth and Seventeenth Centuries', in Chalkin and Havinden (eds.) *Rural Change and Urban Growth 1500–1800*, 1974

J. Raine (ed.) 'Richmond Wills and Inventories', *Surtees Society*, Vol. 26, 1853

H. Ramm, R. Macdowell and E. Mercer, *Shielings and Bastles*, 1970

R. Rawson, *Old Barn Plans*, (New York) 1979

A. D. Rees, *Life in a Welsh Countryside*, 1961

G. B. Rennie, R. Brown and J. Shirreff, *General View of the Agriculture of the West Riding of Yorkshire*, 1794

S. E. Rigold, 'Some Major Kentish Timber Barns', *Archaeologia Cantiana*, Vol. LXXXI, 1967

S. E. Rigold, 'The Distribution of Aisled Timber Barns', *Vernacular Architecture*, Vol. 2, 1971

S. E Rigold, 'Frocester Court Tithe Barn', *Archaeological Journal*, Vol. 134, 1977

D. L. Roberts, 'The Vernacular Buildings of Lincolnshire', *Archaeological Journal*, Vol. 131, 1974

Royal Commission on Historic Monuments (England), *Inventories* for *West Cambridgeshire*, 1968, *Dorset* Vol. II, 1970, *North-East Cambridgeshire*, 1972

P. Ryder, 'Vernacular Buildings in South Yorkshire', *Archaeological Journal*, Vol. 137 (for 1980), 1981

M. E. Seebohm, *The Evolution of the English Farm*, 1952

A. L. Shoemaker, *The Pennsylvania Barn*, 1959 (Kutztown, Pa., USA)

N. Smedley, *Life and Tradition in Suffolk and Northern Essex*, 1976

P. Smith, 'The Long-house and the Laithe-house', in I. Ll. Foster and L. Alcock (eds.) *Culture and Environment*, 1963

P. Smith, *Houses of the Welsh Countryside*, 1975

J. T. Smith, 'The long-house in Monmouthshire: a Reappraisal', in I. Ll. Foster and L. Alcock (eds.) *Culture and Environment*, 1963

J. T. Smith and S. R. Jones, 'The Houses of Breconshire', Parts I to V in *Brycheiniog*, Vols. IX to XIII, 1963 to 1968/9

C. F. Stell, 'Pennine Houses: an Introduction', *Folk Life*, Vol. 3, 1965

H. Stephens, *The Book of the Farm*, 1954

H. Stephens and R. S. Burn, *The Book of Farm Buildings*, 1861

Strickland, *A General View of the Agriculture of the East Riding of Yorkshire*, 1812

C. Taylor, *Fields in the English Landscape*, 1975

J. Thirsk, (ed.), *The Agrarian History of England and Wales*, Vol. IV, 1967

J. Tuke, *General View of the Agriculture of the North Riding of Yorkshire*, 1794

B. Tyson, 'Low Park Barn, Rydal', *and* 'Rydal Hall Farmyard: the Development of a Westmorland Farmstead before 1700', *and* 'Skirwith Hall and Wilton Tenement (Kirkland Hall) the rebuilding of two Cumbrian farmsteads in the Eighteenth Century', in Transactions of the Cumberland and Westmorland Antiquarian and Archaeological Society, NS, Vols. for 1979, 1980, 1981

C. Vancouver, *General View of the Agriculture of Devon*, 1808 (reissued 1969)

J. Vince, *Farms and Farming*, 1971

J. Wade (ed.) *Traditional Kent Buildings*, No. 1, 1980

C. Waistell, *Designs for Agricultural Buildings*, 1827

B. Walker, 'The Influence of Fixed Farm Machinery on Farm Building Design in Eastern Scotland in the Late Eighteenth and Nineteenth Centuries', *The Archaeology of Industrial Scotland* (Scottish Archaeological Forum, 8), 1977

B. Walker, *Farm Buildings in the Grampian Region*, (Grampian Regional Council and the Countryside Commission for Scotland), 1979

J. Waton, 'Upland Houses', *Antiquity*, Vol. XXX, 1956

J. A. Scott Watson and M. E. Hobbs, *Great Farmers*, 1951

J. B. Weller, *Farm Buildings*, 1965

J. Whitaker, 'Two Hebridean Corn Kilns', *Gwerin* Vol. I, 1956–7

T. S. Willan and E. W. Croseley, 'Three Seventeenth Century Yorkshire Surveys', *Yorkshire Archaeological Society Record Series*, Vol. CIV, 1941

E. Wiliam, 'Adeiladau Fferm Traddodiadol yng Nghymru', *Amgueddfa*, 15, 1973

E. Wiliam, 'A Cruck Barn at Hendre Wen, Llanrwst, Denbighshire', *Transactions of the Ancient Monuments Society*, NS Vol. 21, 1976

E. Wiliam, 'Circular Corbelled Pigsties in Wales', Scottish Vernacular Buildings Working Group, *Newsletter*, 6, 1980

E. Wiliam, *Traditional Farm Buildings in North-East Wales, 1550–1900*, 1982

G. H. D. Williams, 'Corn Drying Kilns', *Transactions of the Somerset Archaeological and Natural History Society*, No. 116, 1972

R. D. Wood-Jones, *Traditional Domestic Architecture of the Banbury Region*, 1963

Index

Pages numbered in *italics* indicate illustration by line drawing

Cruck tie, 126
Culvery – see Dovecot
Cumberland, 54, 134
Cumbria, 78, 107, 114, 115, 132
Customary tenant, 20, 22

Dairy, 121, 139
Dartmoor, 34, 104
Derbyshire, 100, 118, 120
Devon, 54, 70, 88, 107, 114, 120, 134
Divots, 137
Domesday Book, 15
Dorset, 88
Dovecots (doocots, culveries) 22, 80–86, *81*, 142
Drying floor (for grain, hops or malt) 95
Dry stone walling, 132
Ducks, 80, 86
Durham, 54
Dutch Barn, 99–100, *101*, 118, 140

Earthen walls – see Clay wall construction
Earth fast posts, 130
East Anglia, 34, 42, 102, 134, 135, 138
Enclosures, 23, 24
English bond brickwork, 135
English garden wall bond brickwork, *133*, 135
Essex, 47, 143

Farmsteads, *32*, 33, 102–122, *103*, *105*
Farmyards, 33, 38, 66–68, 70, 80, 102, *105*, 118, 122, 143
Faughs, 27, 28
Feeding passage, *61*, 62, 74, 76, 104, 109, 139
Feeding trough, *77*
Fermtoun, 27, 28
Field barn, (fieldhouse), 68, 78, 115–120, *116*, 143, 146, 147, 148
First World War, 30, 71, 139
Flemish bond brickwork, 135
Flint wall construction, 85, 123, 132, *133*, 134
Flue, 94–99
Folds, 27
Foldyards, *32*, 33, 35, 66–68, *67*, 71, 73, 102, 115–120, 143
Forebay, 115
France, 115
French Barn, 99–100

Gas engine, 59
Geese, 86
Glover, 84
Granaries, 26, 33, 57, *72*, 74, 87–94, *89*, *90*, 102, 125, 126, 128, 142
Great Coxwell, Berkshire, 35
Great Exhibition, 54

Haddington, East Lothian, 51
Hammels, 71, 73
Hampshire, 135
Hand flail threshing, 36–43, *37*, 55, 104, 118
Harleian system, 65

Harness room, 75
Harrow, Middlesex, 145
Hay barns, 65, 87, 99–100, *101*, 135, 142, 143
Hay loft, *61*, 63, 64, 69, 70, *72*, 74, 78, 99, 135, 139
Hayrack, 62, *63*, 68, 70, *72*, 74
Head-dyke, 27, 28
Heifers, 66, 73, 118
Hemmel – see Shelter shed
Hens – see Poultry
Herefordshire, 95, 98, 129, 147
High farming, 25, 26
Hog-houses, 78
Hop drying kiln – see Oast house
Hop house – see Oast House
Hops, 95–98
Horse-engine, 53–55
Horse-engine house, *50*, 54, 55
Horse-hair blanket, 94, 97
Horse power, 53, 55, 73, 141
Horses, 25, 26, 28, 54, 60, 73–75, 91
Hot air engine, 59

Infield, 18, 27

Jointed crucks, *124*, 125, 134

Kent, 43, 47, 95, 98, 104
Kiln floor, *93*, 99
Kilns, 87, *93*, 94–99, 142
Kiln tiles, *93*, 94, 99
King post roof construction, 130, *131*
Kirktoun, 28
Knee brace, *127*

Lacock, Wilts., 144
Laithe-houses, 102, *103*, 104–109, *105*, *106*
Lake District, 34, 104, 114, 134
Lancashire, 45, 114, 130
Lancashire Barn, 109–11, *110*, 114, 143
Lectern dovecot, 84
Leicester Guildhall, 47
Leicestershire, 47, 118, 130, 134
Leigh Court, Worcs., 126
Lever, William Hesketh (Lord Leverhulme), 145
Liming, 24
Lincolnshire, 130, 147
Linhay, *69*, 69–70, 87
Lleyn Peninsula, 134
Log wall construction, 132
London, 98
Longhouse, 19, 66, 102, *103*, 104–109, *105*, *106*
Loose boxes, 71, 73, 75, *77*, 78, 86, 118, 130
Lower Peover, Cheshire, 47
Lune Valley, 114

Malt, 94
Malting kilns, 98–99
Maltings, *96*, 98–99, 142
Manger, 62, *63*, 68, *72*, 74
Manure passage, *61*, 62, 76, 104, 109